T0163639

William Nealy

MENASHA RIDGE PRESS
Your Guide to the Outdoors Since 1982
an imprint of AdventureKEEN

Kayaks to Hell

Printed in the United States of America

Published by
MENASHA RIDGE PRESS
Your Guide to the Outdoors Since 1982
an imprint of AdventureKEEN

2204 First Ave. S., Ste. 102
Birmingham, Alabama 35233
800-678-7006, FAX 877-374-9016
adventurewithkeen.com

ISBN 978-1-63404-366-3 (pbk); ISBN 978-1-63404-367-0 (ebook)

PUBLISHER'S NOTE

What you hold in your hands is a book of William Nealy's art, pulled from the gnarliest Class VI rapids of time . . . almost lost forever.

But now Nealy's zany illustrations have been bound and bandaged together in a new monumental collection, including books and cartoons long out of print. Nealy's full-speed downhill no-holds-barred art has been reset and brought back to life like never before.

This is the craziest collection of cartoons since Nealy first put paddle to water and pen to paper. The result is a hilarious slice of the outdoor community as extreme and cutting as Nealy was himself.

Many of the illustrations have not been seen since they were first published. Now they're back and will certainly delight old and new Nealy fans alike. We've taken care to make sure the flow of Nealy's stories and illustrations work just as well in this new format as they did when they were first published years ago.

We are proud at Menasha Ridge Press and AdventureKEEN to help return Nealy's art and irreverent illustrations to the bookshelf. Nealy had a gift for teaching, storytelling, and capturing the beauty of the rivers he sketched and the people he loved. His humorous approach to telling the twisted tales of paddlers, mountain bikers, hikers, campers, inline skaters, and skiers everywhere is a gift to all participating in the weird, wonderful world of outdoor sports.

You can learn more about William, his art, and his many books at thewilliamnealy.com.

SINCERELY,
THE MENASHA RIDGE
PRESS TEAM

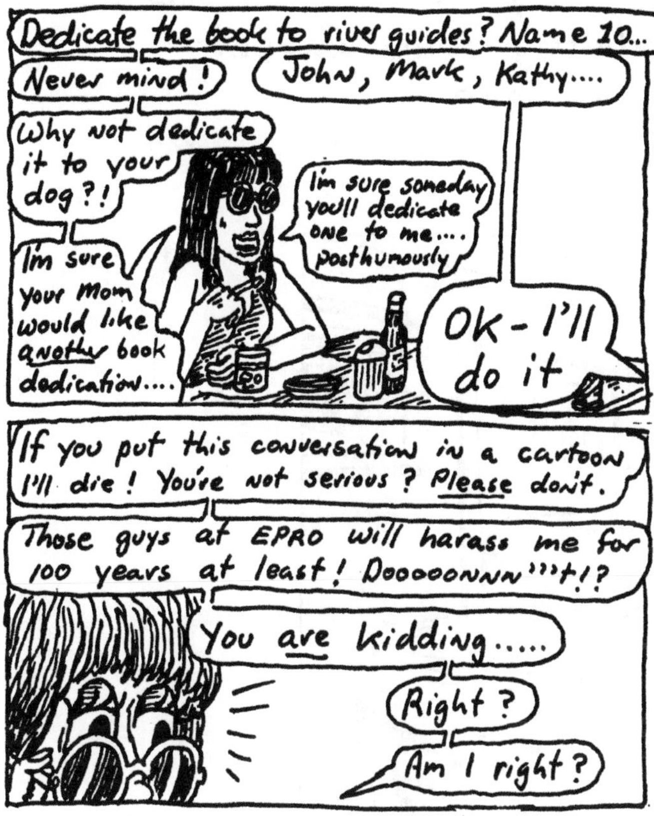
Dedicate the book to river guides? Name 10...
Never mind!
John, Mark, Kathy....
Why not dedicate it to your dog?!
I'm sure someday you'll dedicate one to me.... posthumously
I'm sure your mom would like another book dedication....
OK - I'll do it
If you put this conversation in a cartoon I'll die! You're not serious? Please don't.
Those guys at EPRO will harass me for 100 years at least! Dooooonnn'''t!?
You are kidding.....
Right?
Am I right?

This book is dedicated to my "special friend", Holland Wallace

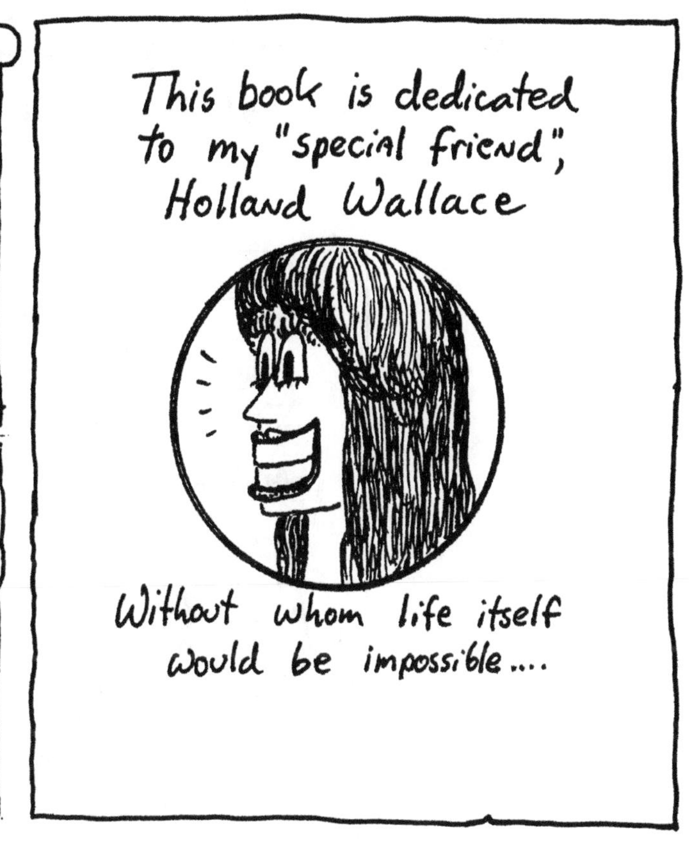

Without whom life itself would be impossible....

Acknowledgements

Thanks to Bob Sehlinger, Jeff & Lani Cartier, Henry & Donna Unger, David Vernon, Kathy Cook, Larry Nahmias, Holly "After-all-I-did-edit-your-book-*too*" Wallace, John Barber and all trout everywhere.

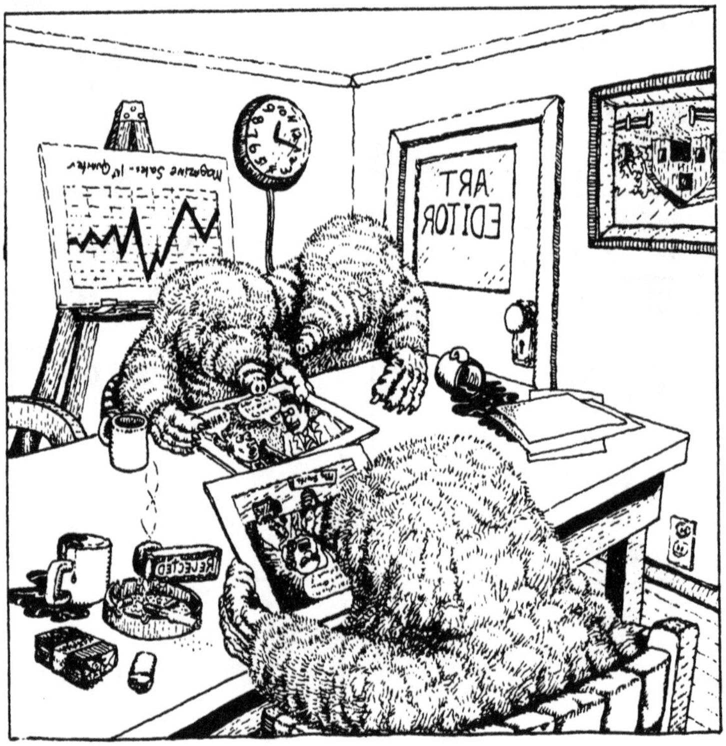
ART
EDITOR
REJECTED

Leopards break into the temple and drink to the dregs what is in the sacrificial pitchers; this is repeated over and over again; finally it can be calculated in advance, and it becomes part of the ceremony.

Franz Kafka

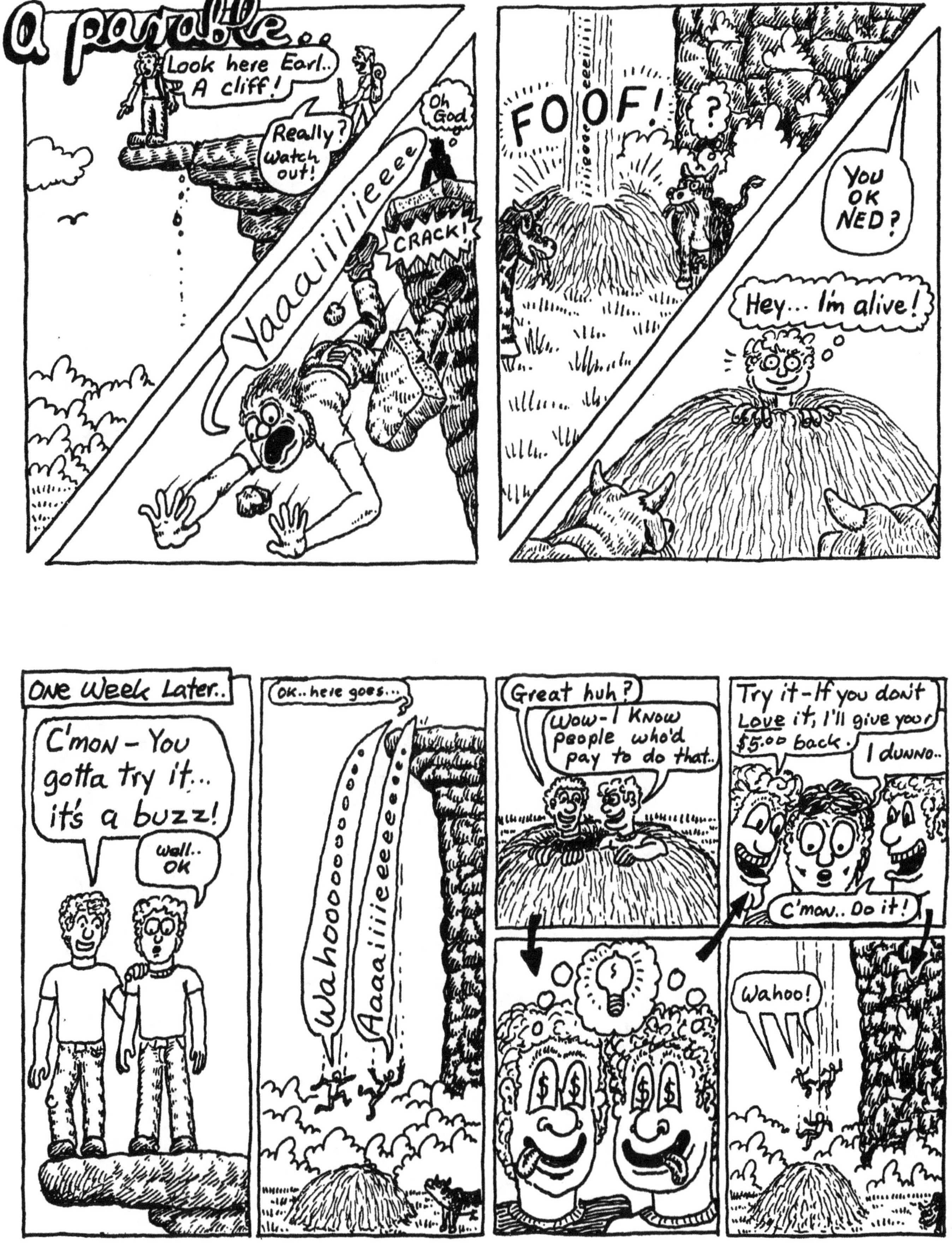

A parable...
Look here Earl.. A cliff!
Really? Watch out!
Oh God
Yaaaiiiiieeee
CRACK!
FOOF!
?
YOU OK NED?
Hey... I'm alive!
ONE Week Later..
C'MON - You gotta try it... it's a buzz!
well.. OK
OK.. here goes...
Wahoooooooo
Aaaaiiiieeeee
Great huh?
Wow - I KNOW people who'd pay to do that..
Try it - If you don't Love it, I'll give your $5.00 back.
I DUNNO..
C'MON.. Do it!
Wahoo!

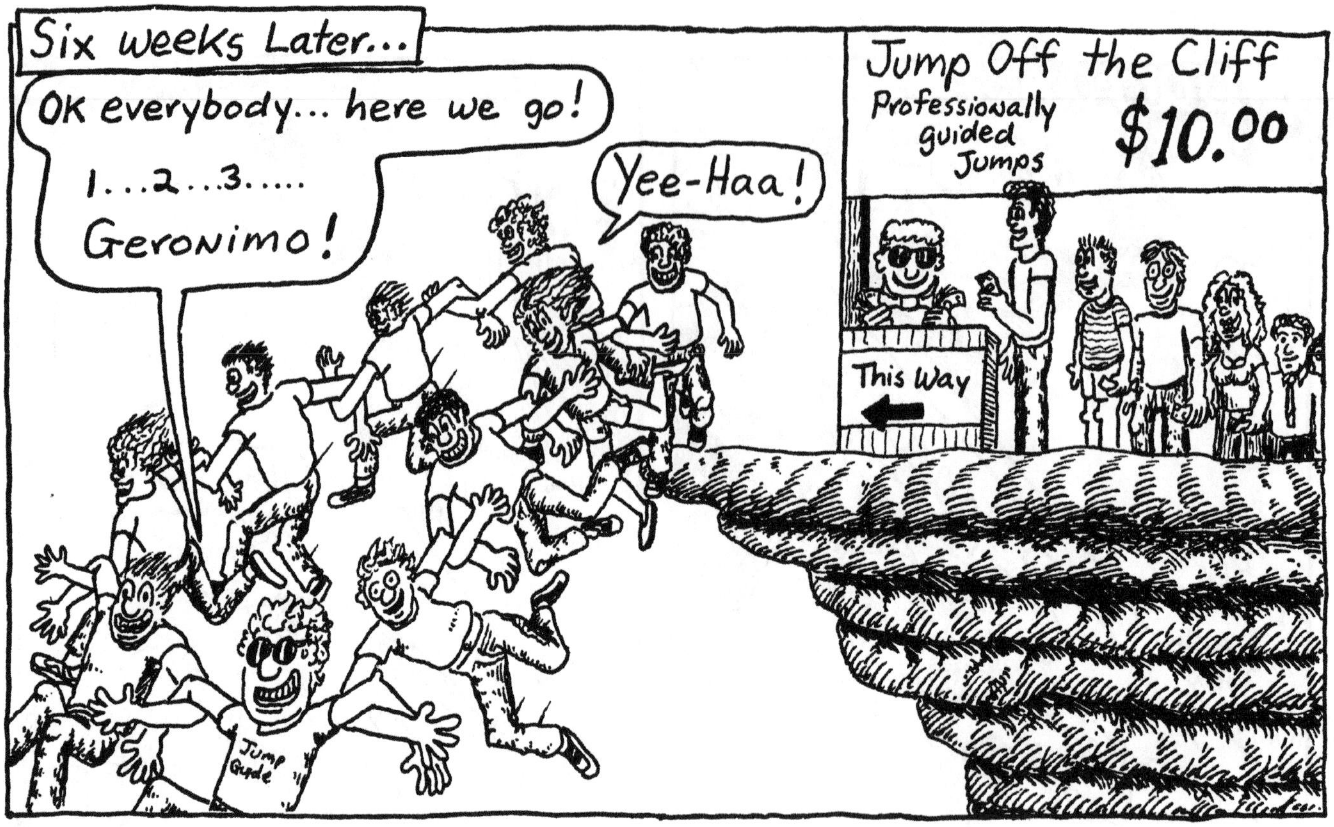
Six weeks Later...
OK everybody... here we go!
1...2...3.....
Geronimo!
Yee-Haa!
Jump Off the Cliff
Professionally guided Jumps
$10.00
This Way
Jump Guide

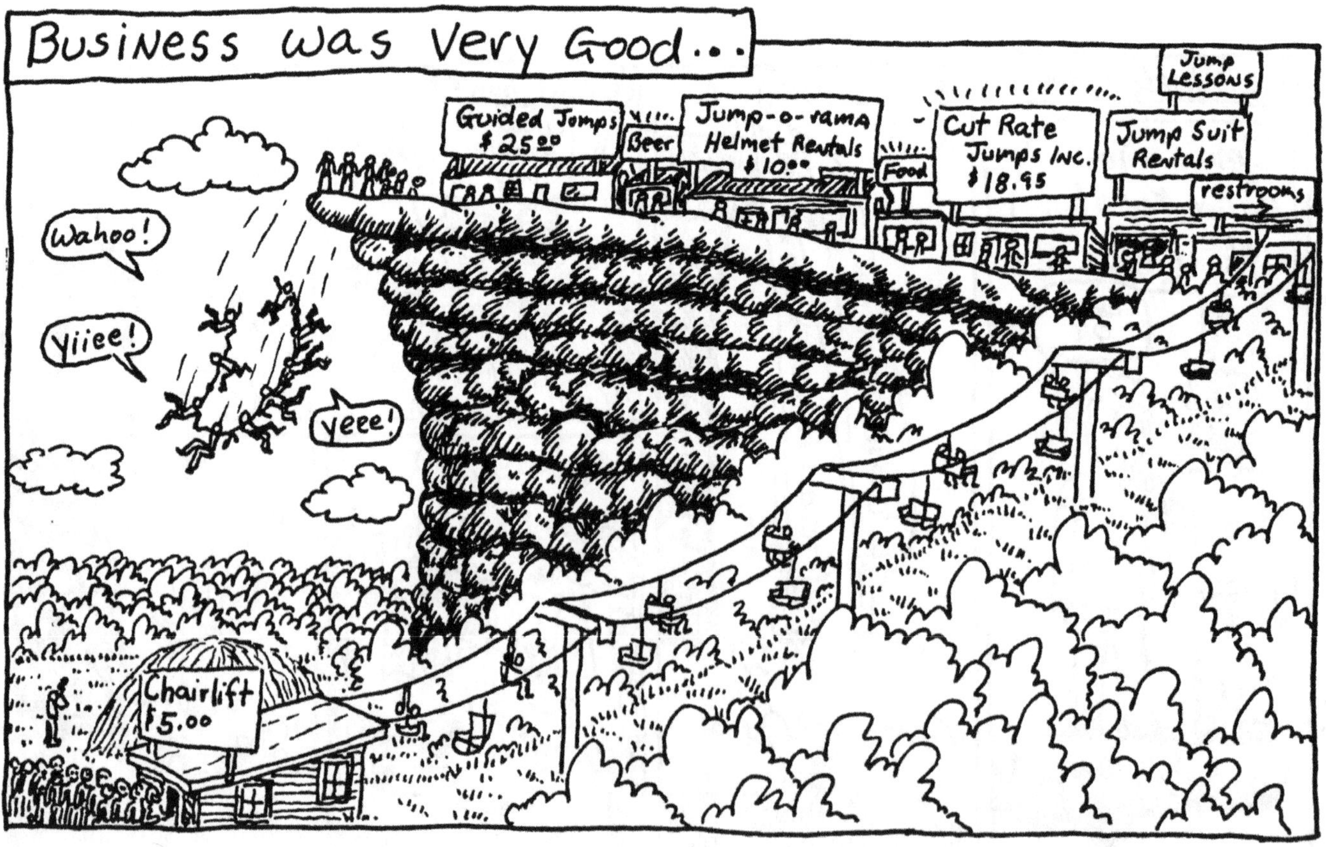
Business was Very Good...
Jump Lessons
Guided Jumps $25.00
Beer
Jump-o-rama Helmet Rentals $10.00
Food
Cut Rate Jumps Inc. $18.95
Jump Suit Rentals
restrooms
Wahoo!
Yiiee!
yeee!
Chairlift $5.00

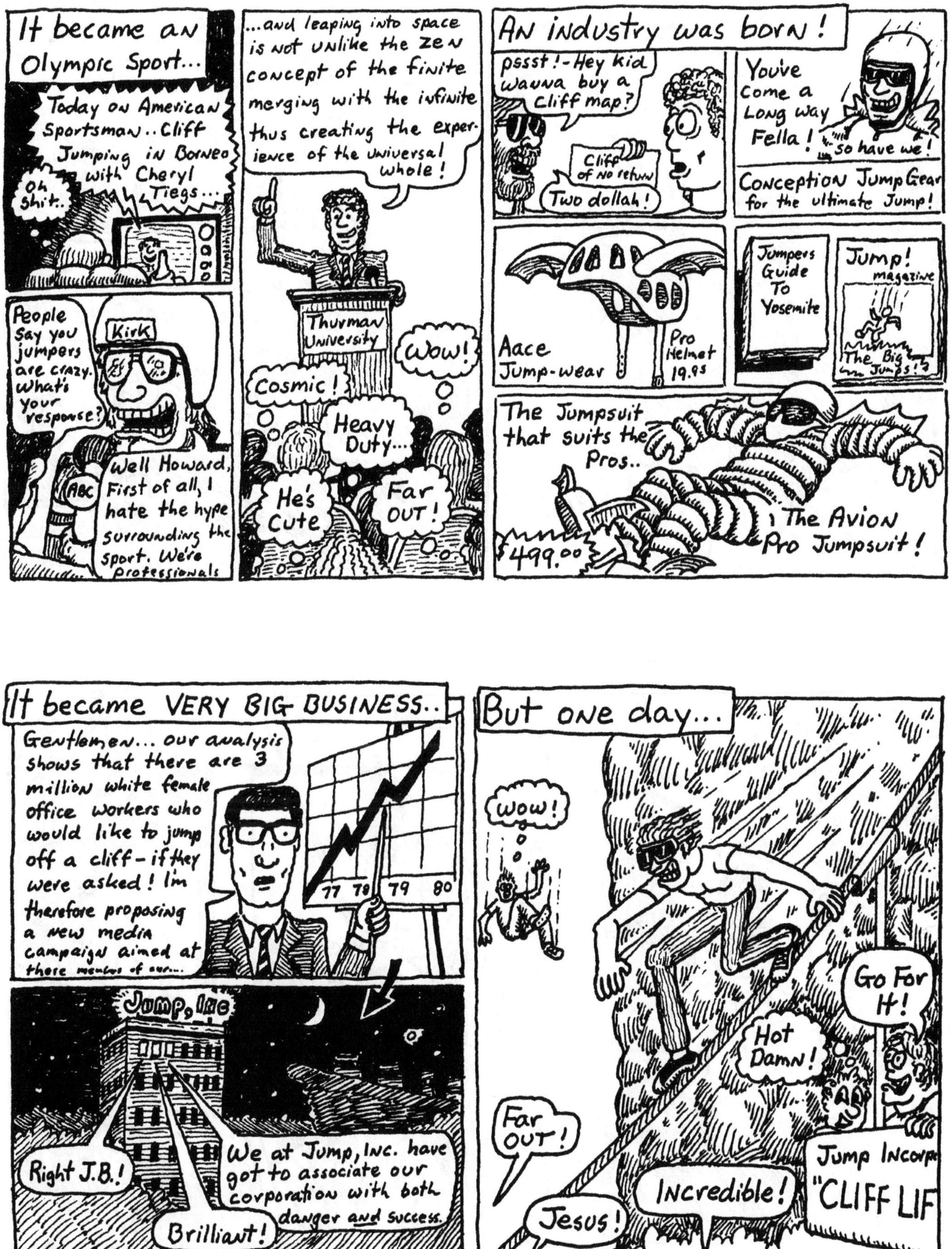
It became an Olympic Sport...
Today on American Sportsman.. Cliff Jumping in Borneo with Cheryl Tiegs...
Oh shit..
...and leaping into space is not unlike the zen concept of the finite merging with the infinite thus creating the experience of the universal whole!
Thurman University
Wow!
Cosmic!
Heavy Duty...
He's Cute
Far OUT!
People say you jumpers are crazy. What's your response?
Kirk
ABC
Well Howard, First of all, I hate the hype surrounding the sport. We're professionals
An industry was born!
pssst!-Hey kid wanna buy a Cliff map?
Cliff of no return
Two dollah!
You've come a Long way Fella!
so have we!
Conception Jump Gear for the ultimate Jump!
Aace Jump-wear
Pro Helmet 19.95
Jumpers Guide To Yosemite
Jump! magazine
The Big Jumps!
The Jumpsuit that suits the Pros..
The Avion Pro Jumpsuit!
499.00
It became VERY BIG BUSINESS..
Gentlemen... our analysis shows that there are 3 million white female office workers who would like to jump off a cliff - if they were asked! I'm therefore proposing a new media campaign aimed at
77 78 79 80
Jump, Inc
Right J.B.!
Brilliant!
We at Jump, Inc. have got to associate our corporation with both danger and success.
But one day...
Wow!
Go For It!
Hot Damn!
Far OUT!
Jesus!
Incredible!
Jump Incorp
"CLIFF LIF

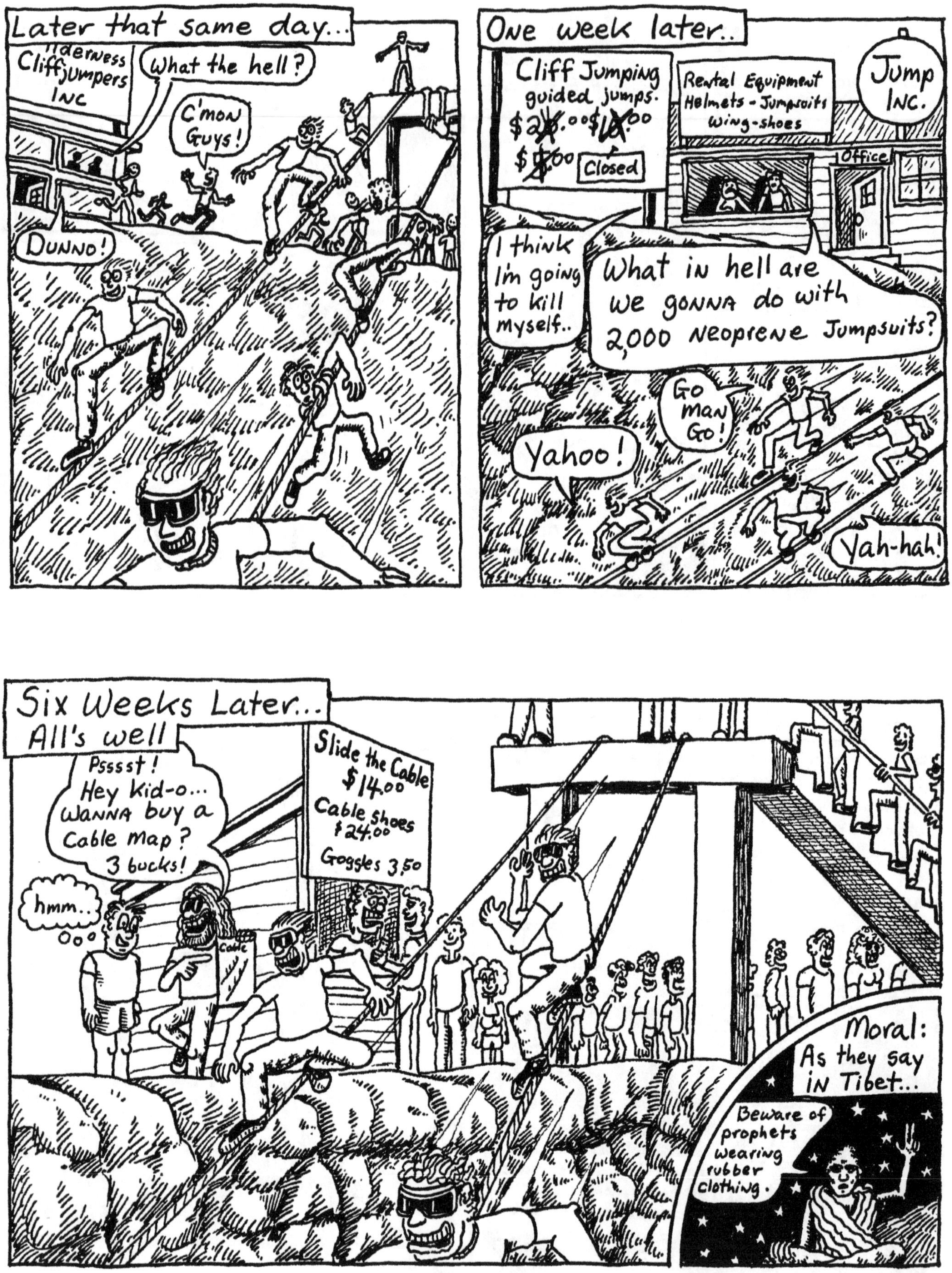

Later that same day...
lderness Cliffjumpers INC
What the hell?
C'mon Guys!
Dunno!
One week later..
Cliff Jumping guided jumps.
Closed
Rental Equipment Helmets - Jumpsuits wing-shoes
Jump INC.
Office
I think I'm going to kill myself..
What in hell are we gonna do with 2,000 neoprene Jumpsuits?
Go man Go!
Yahoo!
Yah-hah!
Six Weeks Later...
All's well
Psssst! Hey kid-o... wanna buy a Cable map? 3 bucks!
hmm..
Slide the Cable $14.00
Cable shoes $24.00
Goggles 3.50
Cable
Moral: As they say in Tibet...
Beware of prophets wearing rubber clothing.

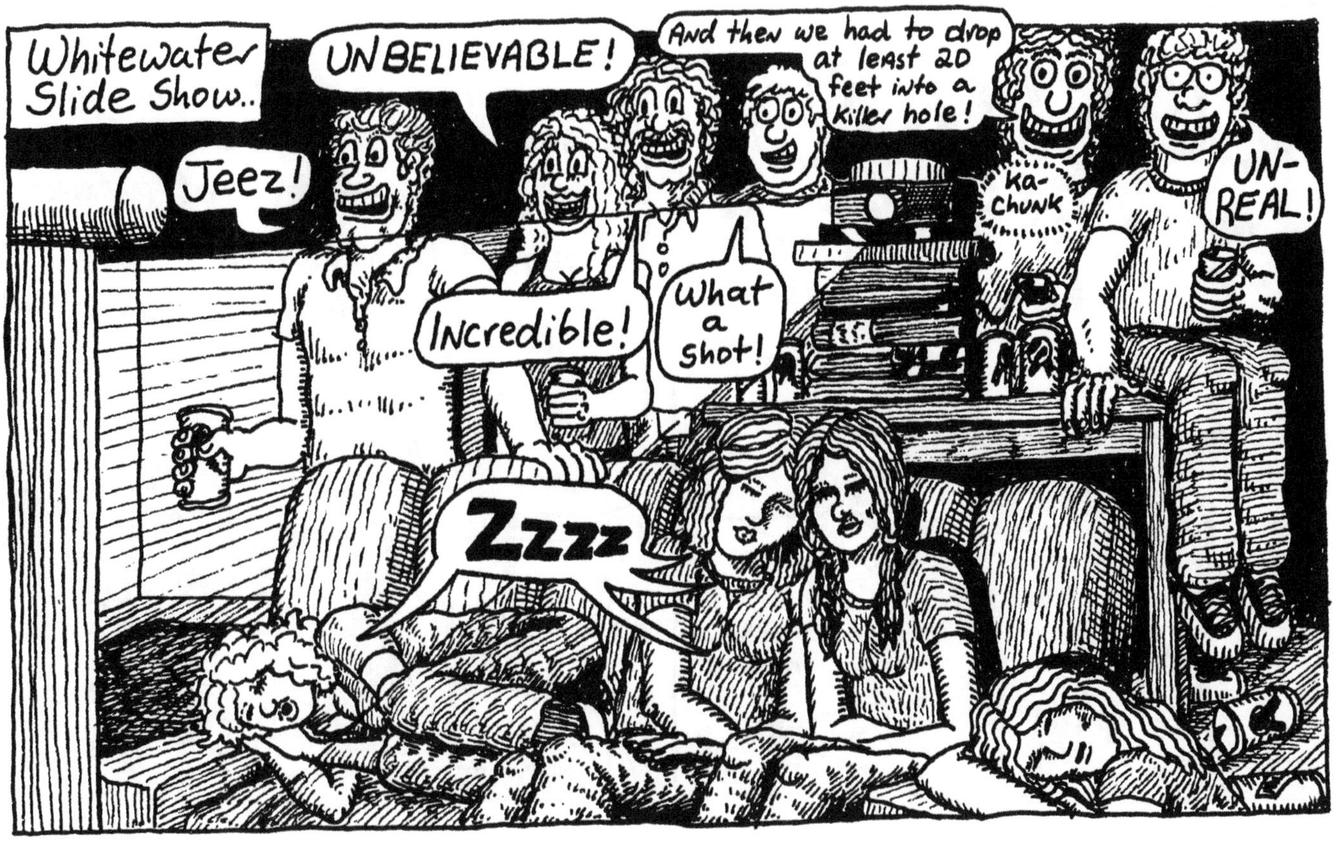

Whitewater Slide Show..
UNBELIEVABLE!
And then we had to drop at least 20 feet into a killer hole!
Jeez!
Ka-CHUNK
UN-REAL!
Incredible!
What a shot!
Zzzz

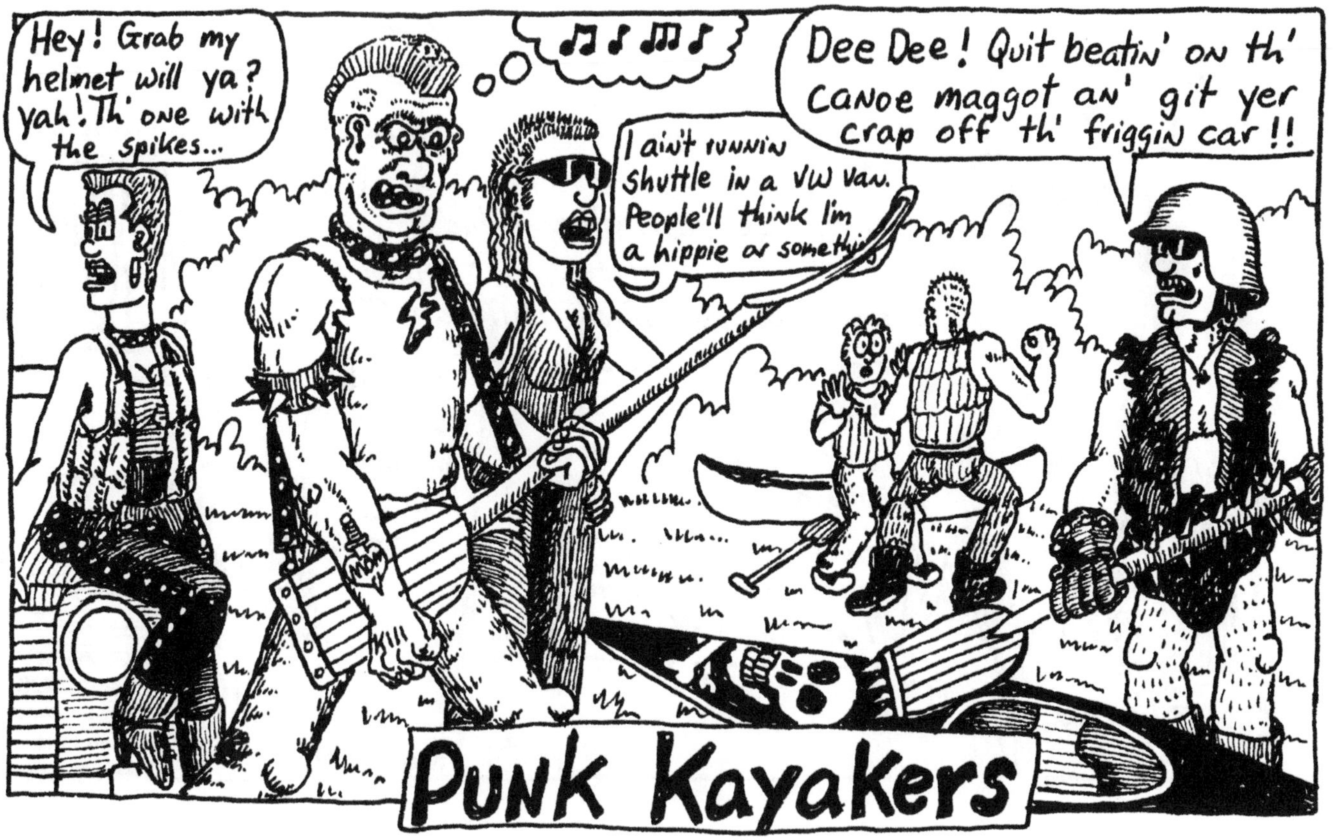

Hey! Grab my helmet will ya? yah! Th' one with the spikes...
♫♪♫♪
Dee Dee! Quit beatin' on th' canoe maggot an' git yer crap off th' friggin car!!
I ain't runnin shuttle in a VW van. People'll think I'm a hippie or someth
Punk Kayakers

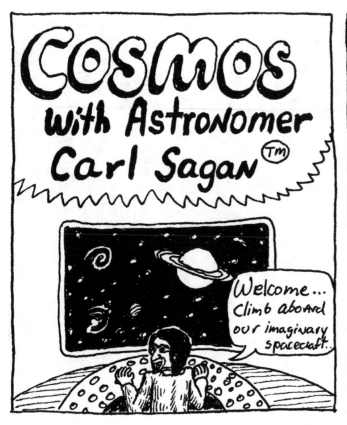

COSMOS
with Astronomer
Carl Sagan(TM)
Welcome... Climb aboard our imaginary spacecraft.
This week we will be exploring a peculiar section of our local universe. It's a place of strange creatures, of inexplicable behavior patterns, of unusual physical laws... We're going to a little-known area on our planet... to a place called "river world"!
The Following Week...
This evening, Cosmos will be examining the principle of Entropy - the universal tendency of all systems, large and small, to fall into total disorder. We have traveled to the mountains of North Carolina, created millions and millions of years ago when the European plate collided with the North American plate... but that's another story and an entirely different discipline.... Assisting us in our demonstration of Entropy will be a river runner who appears to have had considerable experience with entropy already... Let's begin the experiment.
Hi Everybody!

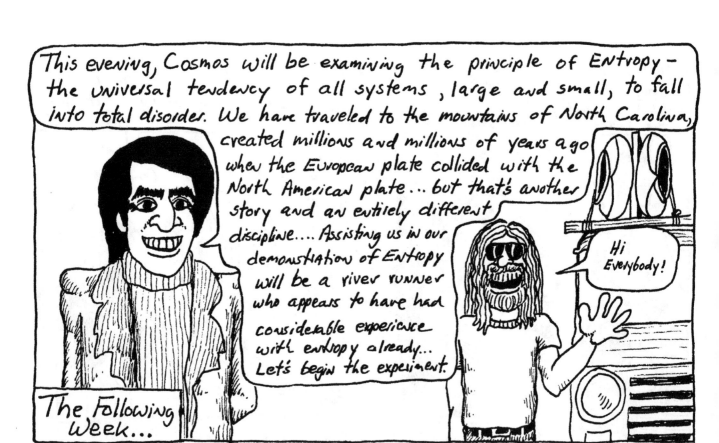

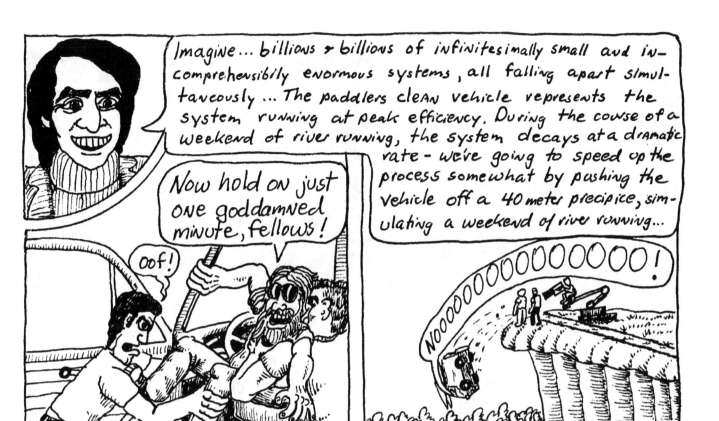

Imagine... billions & billions of infinitesimally small and incomprehensibly enormous systems, all falling apart simultaneously ... The paddlers clean vehicle represents the system running at peak efficiency. During the course of a weekend of river running, the system decays at a dramatic rate - we're going to speed up the process somewhat by pushing the vehicle off a 40 meter precipice, simulating a weekend of river running...

Now hold on just one goddamned minute, fellows!

Oof!

NOOOOOOOOOOOOOOOO!

KA WHUMP!

Oooohhhh....

We carefully photograph the inside of the vehicle or "system" and compare it to a photograph taken after a previous weekend of river running and....

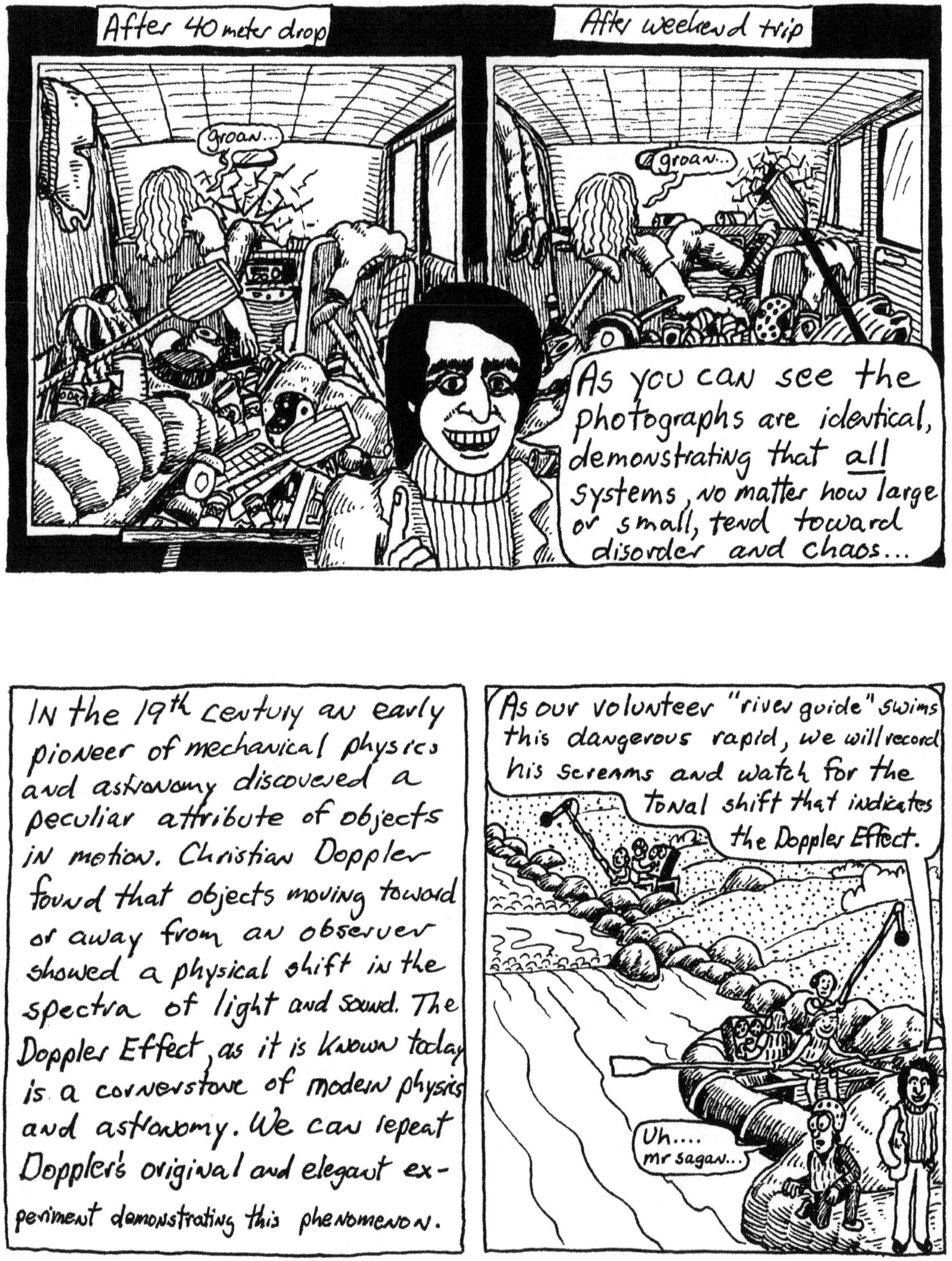
After 40 meter drop
groan...
After weekend trip
groan...
As you can see the photographs are identical, demonstrating that all systems, no matter how large or small, tend toward disorder and chaos...
In the 19th century an early pioneer of mechanical physics and astronomy discovered a peculiar attribute of objects in motion. Christian Doppler found that objects moving toward or away from an observer showed a physical shift in the spectra of light and sound. The Doppler Effect, as it is known today is a cornerstone of modern physics and astronomy. We can repeat Doppler's original and elegant experiment demonstrating this phenomenon.
As our volunteer "river guide" swims this dangerous rapid, we will record his screams and watch for the tonal shift that indicates the Doppler Effect.
Uh.... mr sagan...

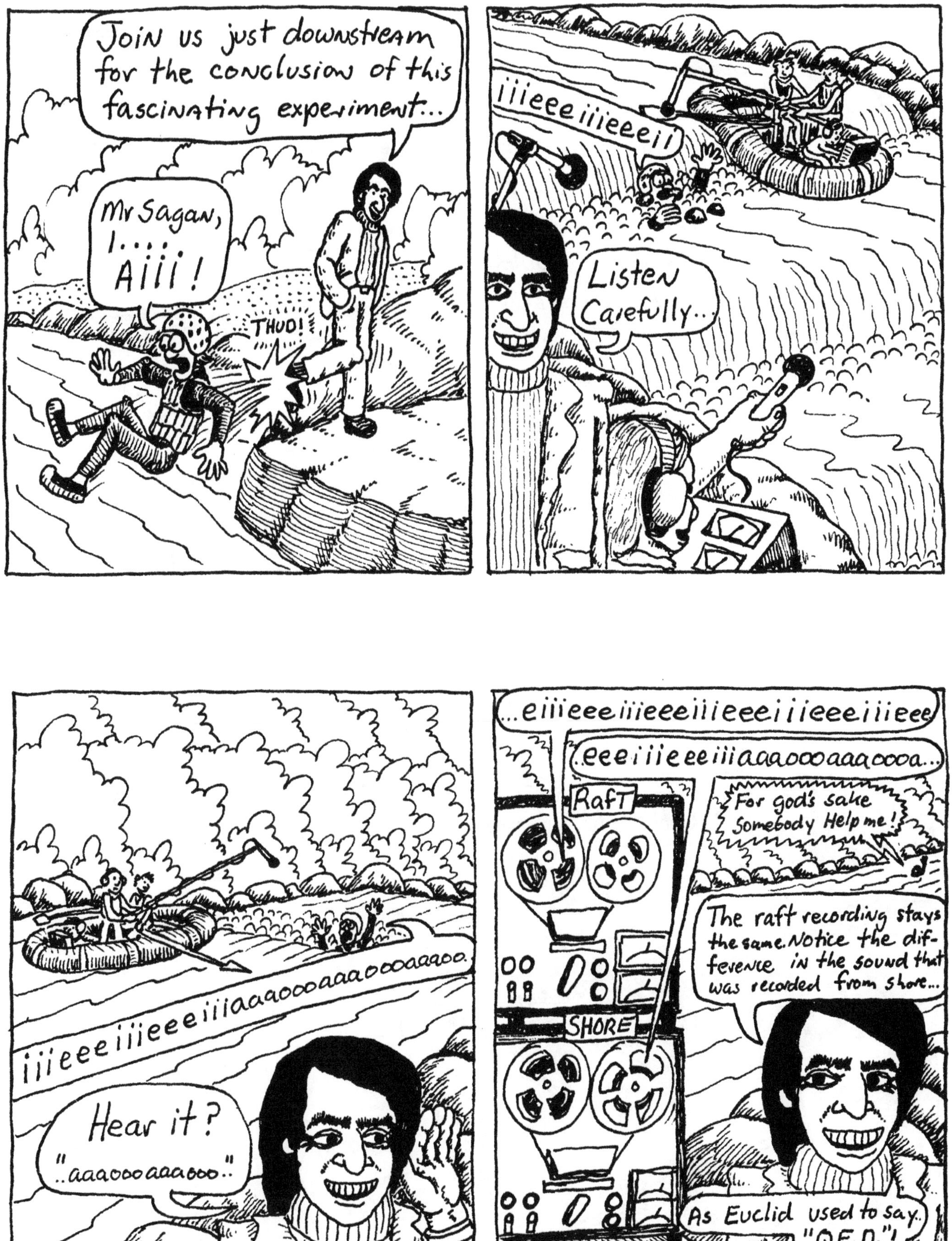
Join us just downstream for the conclusion of this fascinating experiment...
Mr Sagan, I.... Aiii!
THUD!
iiieeeiiieeeii
Listen Carefully..
iiieeeiiieeeiiiaaaoooaaaoooaaaoo.
Hear it? "..aaaoooaaaooo.."
...eiiieeeiiieeeiiieeeiiieeeiiieee
.eeeiiieeeiiiaaaoooaaaoooa...
Raft
For god's sake Somebody Help me!
SHORE
The raft recording stays the same. Notice the difference in the sound that was recorded from shore...
As Euclid used to say.. "Q.E.D."!

Our next experiment takes us to the mountains of West Virginia, to a bridge high above the New River. Perched over 870 feet above the river, this single span arch bridge should provide an excellent living-laboratory for a demonstration of Kinetic Energy. As you may recall Kinetic Energy of any object is equal to mass times velocity squared times .5. As you can see, the kinetic energy of an object increases exponentially...

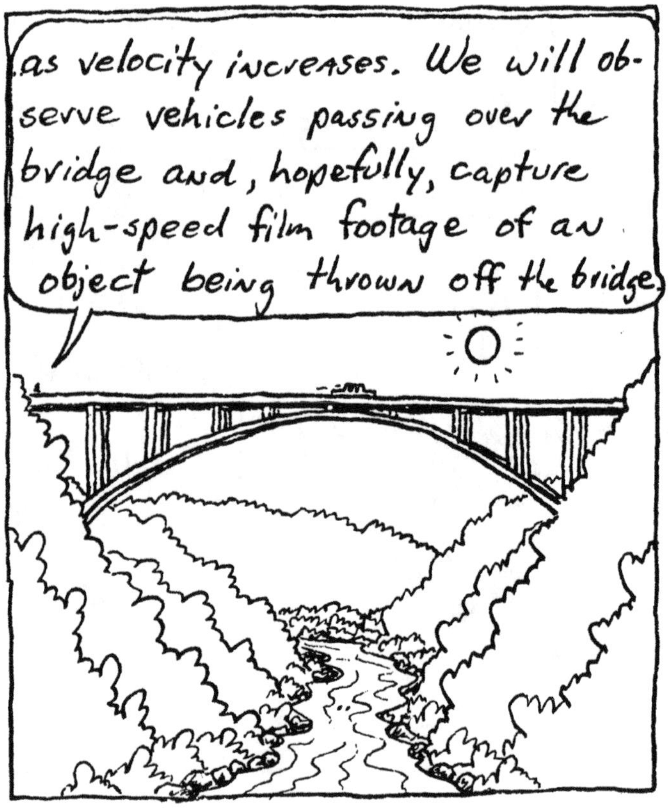
as velocity increases. We will observe vehicles passing over the bridge and, hopefully, capture high-speed film footage of an object being thrown off the bridge.

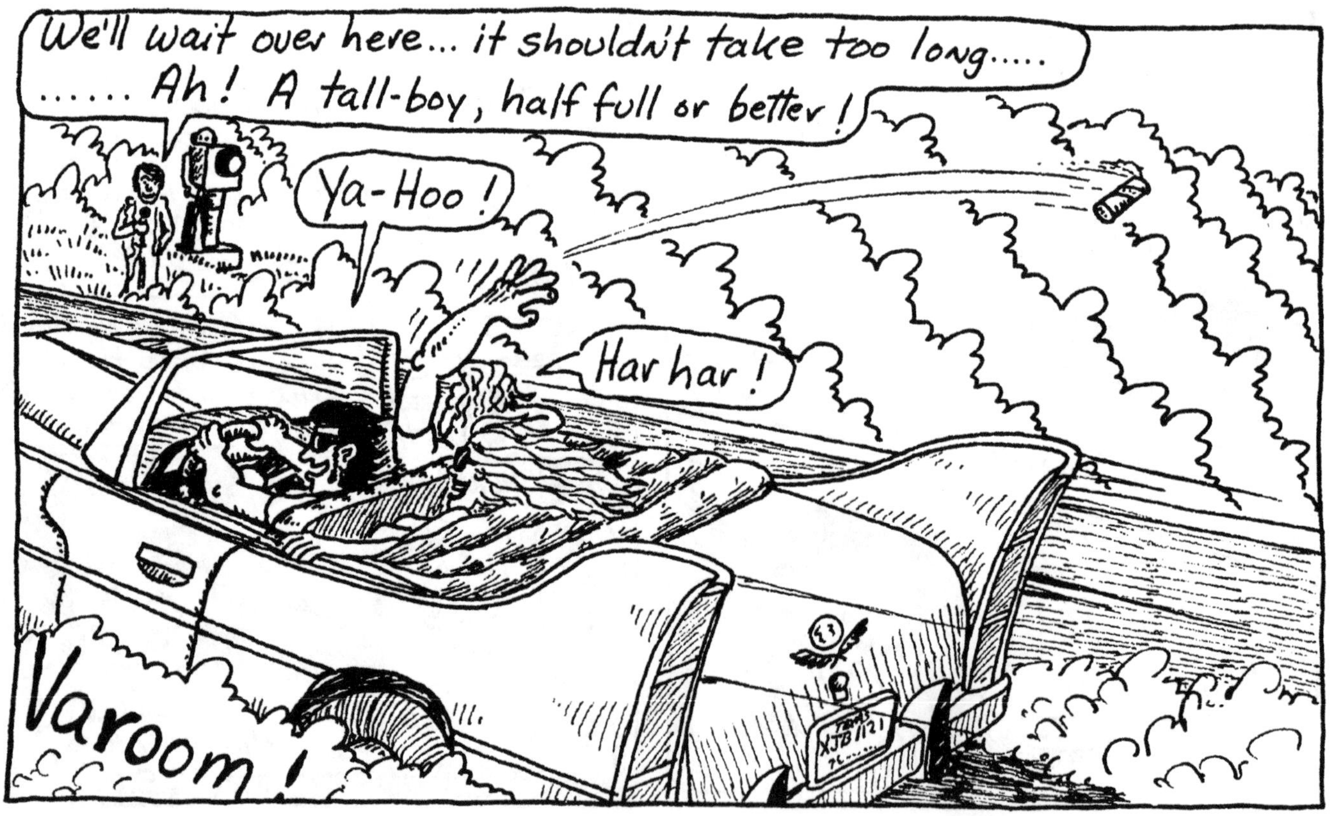
We'll wait over here... it shouldn't take too long..... ...... Ah! A tall-boy, half full or better!
Ya-Hoo!
Har har!
Varoom!

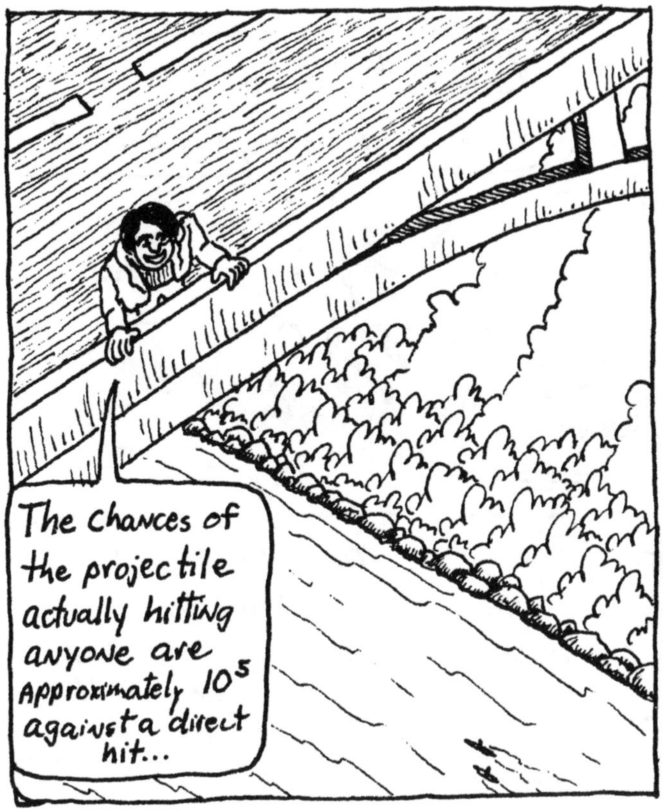
The chances of the projectile actually hitting anyone are approximately 10^5 against a direct hit...

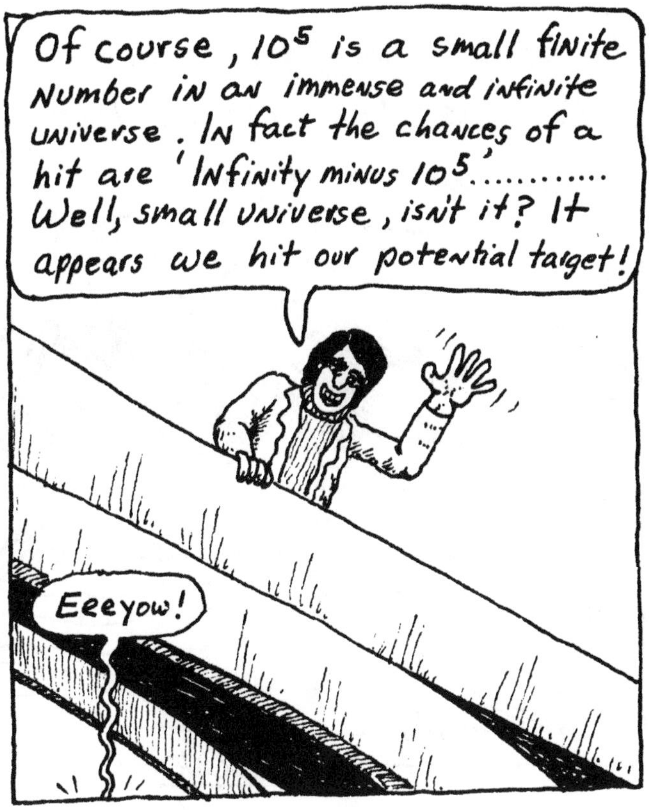
Of course, 10^5 is a small finite number in an immense and infinite universe. In fact the chances of a hit are 'Infinity minus 10^5'.......... Well, small universe, isn't it? It appears we hit our potential target!
Eeeyow!

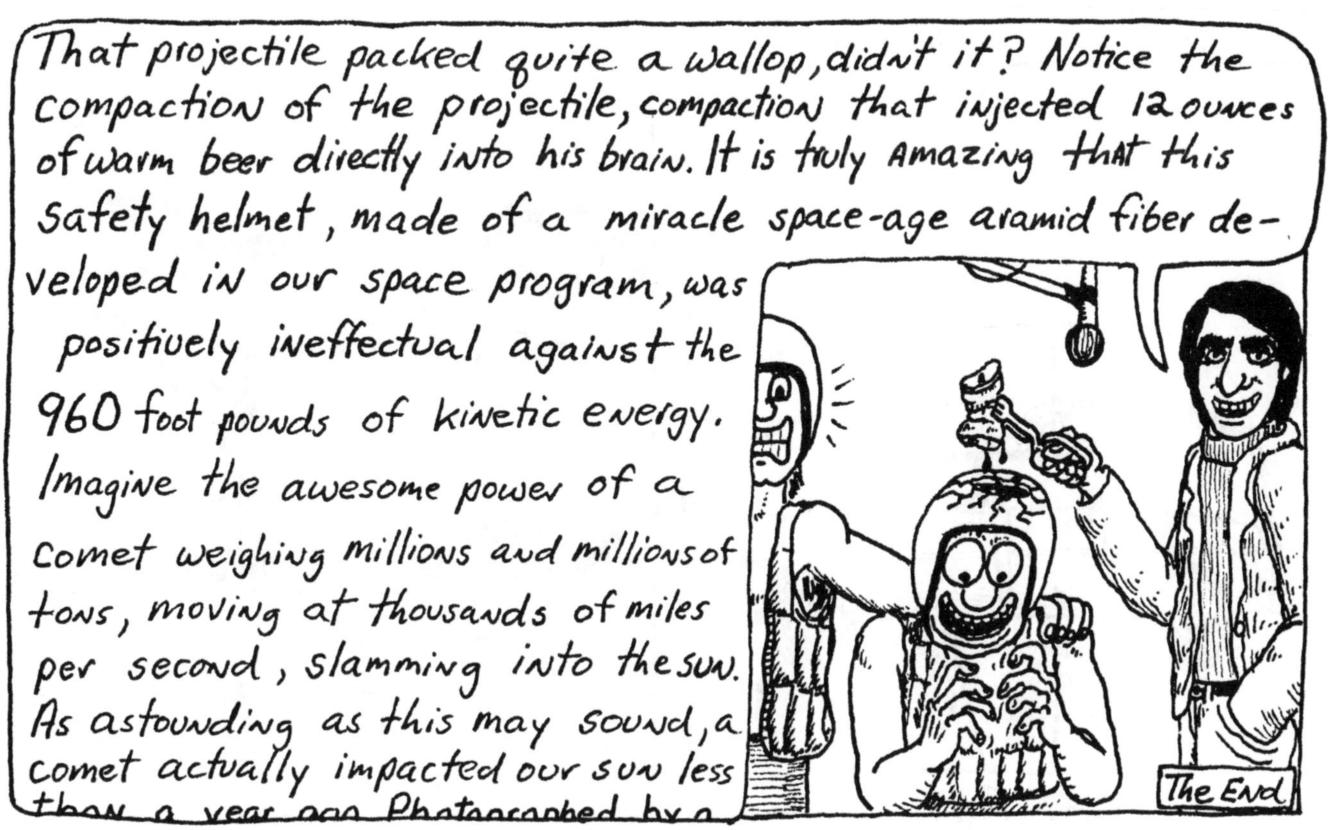
That projectile packed quite a wallop, didn't it? Notice the compaction of the projectile, compaction that injected 12 ounces of warm beer directly into his brain. It is truly amazing that this safety helmet, made of a miracle space-age aramid fiber developed in our space program, was positively ineffectual against the 960 foot pounds of kinetic energy. Imagine the awesome power of a comet weighing millions and millions of tons, moving at thousands of miles per second, slamming into the sun. As astounding as this may sound, a comet actually impacted our sun less than a year ago. Photographed by a
The End

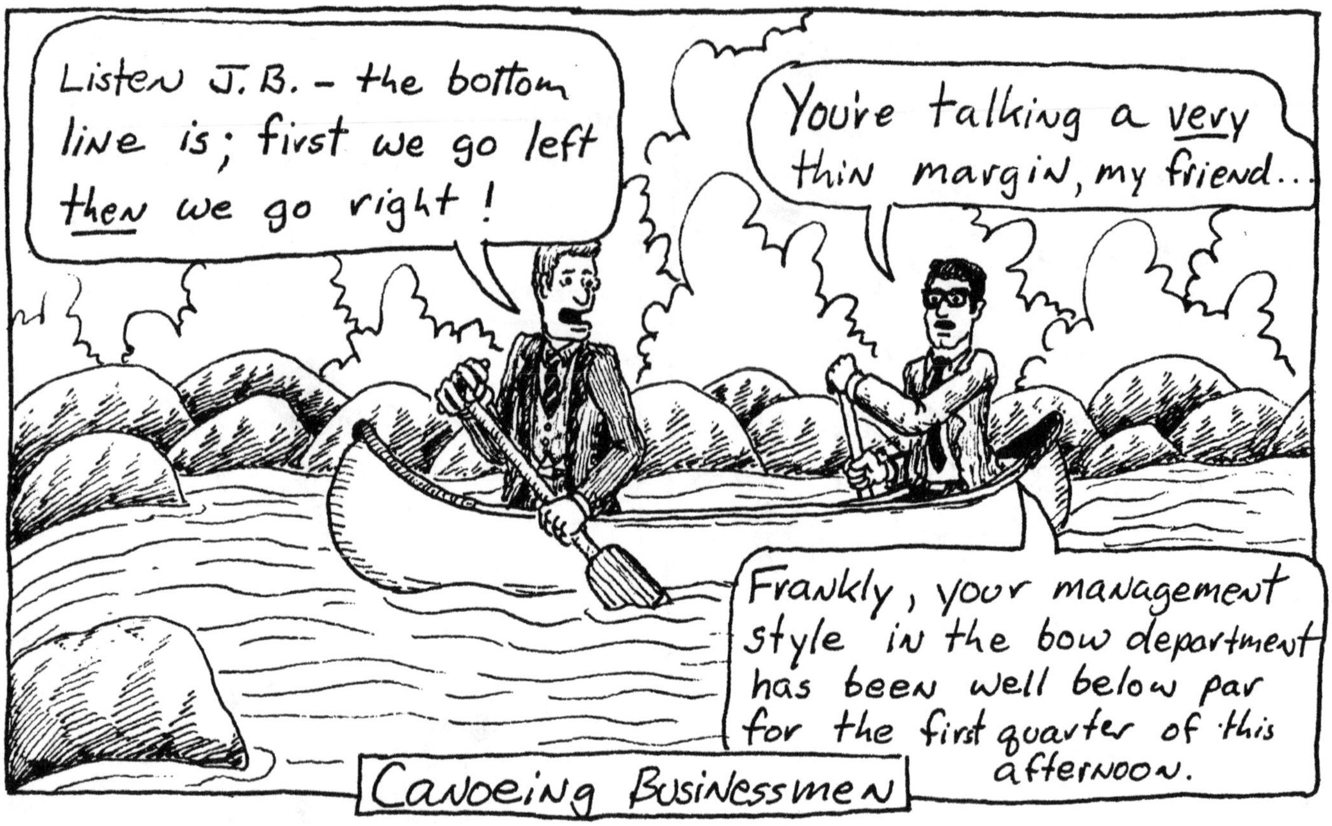
Listen J.B. – the bottom line is; first we go left then we go right!
You're talking a very thin margin, my friend...
Frankly, your management style in the bow department has been well below par for the first quarter of this afternoon.
Canoeing Businessmen

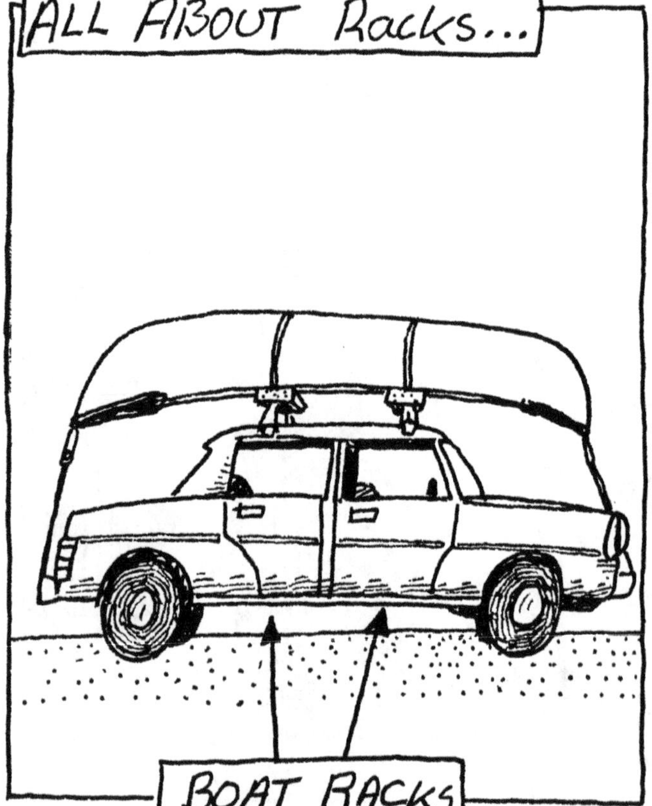
ALL ABOUT Racks...
BOAT RACKS

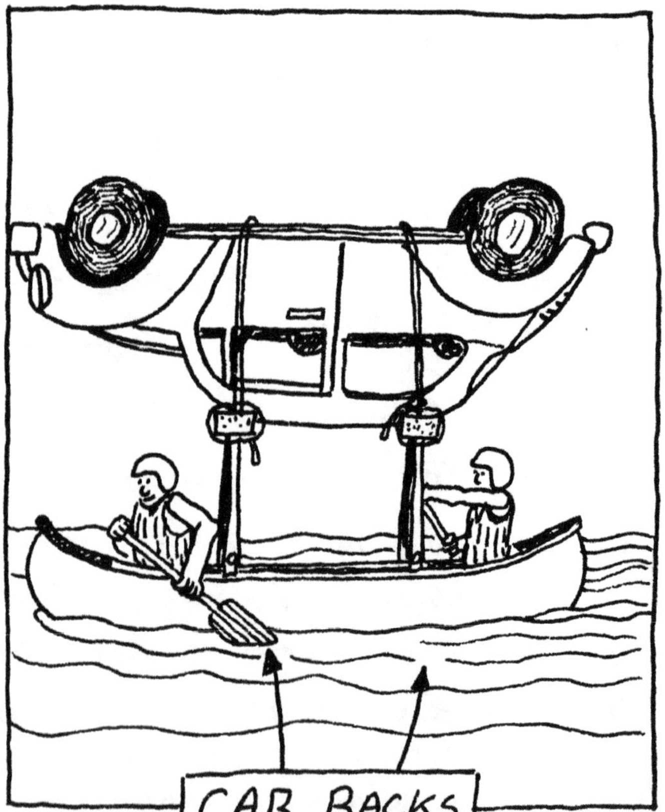
CAR RACKS

How to pick up a river person..

"Hey.. weren't we in the same affinity group at the Diablo Canyon Nuke Rally?"

Lines that frequently work...

① "Great ender - I wish _I_ could do that."

② "Hey babe, ever paddle tandem canoe in Class IV water? Want to?"

③ "I simply _love_ the new North Face dome tents...So aesthetic... beautiful lines...structurally un-surpassed! Oh..You _have_ one..."

④ "Want to run Big Laurel tomorrow? Small group... maybe just you and me ... You can handle it, NO PROBLEM! I _hate_ big groups..."

⑤ "I have a gas credit card...."

⑥ "It's really wonderful to talk to someone who doesn't have to talk about whitewater all the time."

⑦ "I _hate_ these crowded camp-grounds. So noisy.. so impersonal... There's a nice campsite down by the creek that's ....quieter."

⑧ "I see what you're saying... the post impressionist painters were exploring the dialectic of objects and time in totally non-spatial relationships. Wow, that's fascinating!"

⑨ Oooh! I'd _love_ to see your slides of the Grand — I'll bet that was incredible! Now? Great!"

How NOT to pick up a river person

① "I don't give backrubs. Ever!"

② "I found the Lord this Spring!"

③ "Can't you talk about anything except boats? Boats are _so_ boring!"

④ "They weren't really warts...it went away the next day.... honest!"

General Put-off Approaches..

① Talk about El Salvador.

② Play the Sex Pistols LOUD on the way to the campground.

③ Throw up in his/her car.

④ Talk incessantly about your boyfriend /girlfriend/husband/wife/housemate.

Owed to B. Kliban

River Accessories
from
S & M River
Tours & Supplies . . .

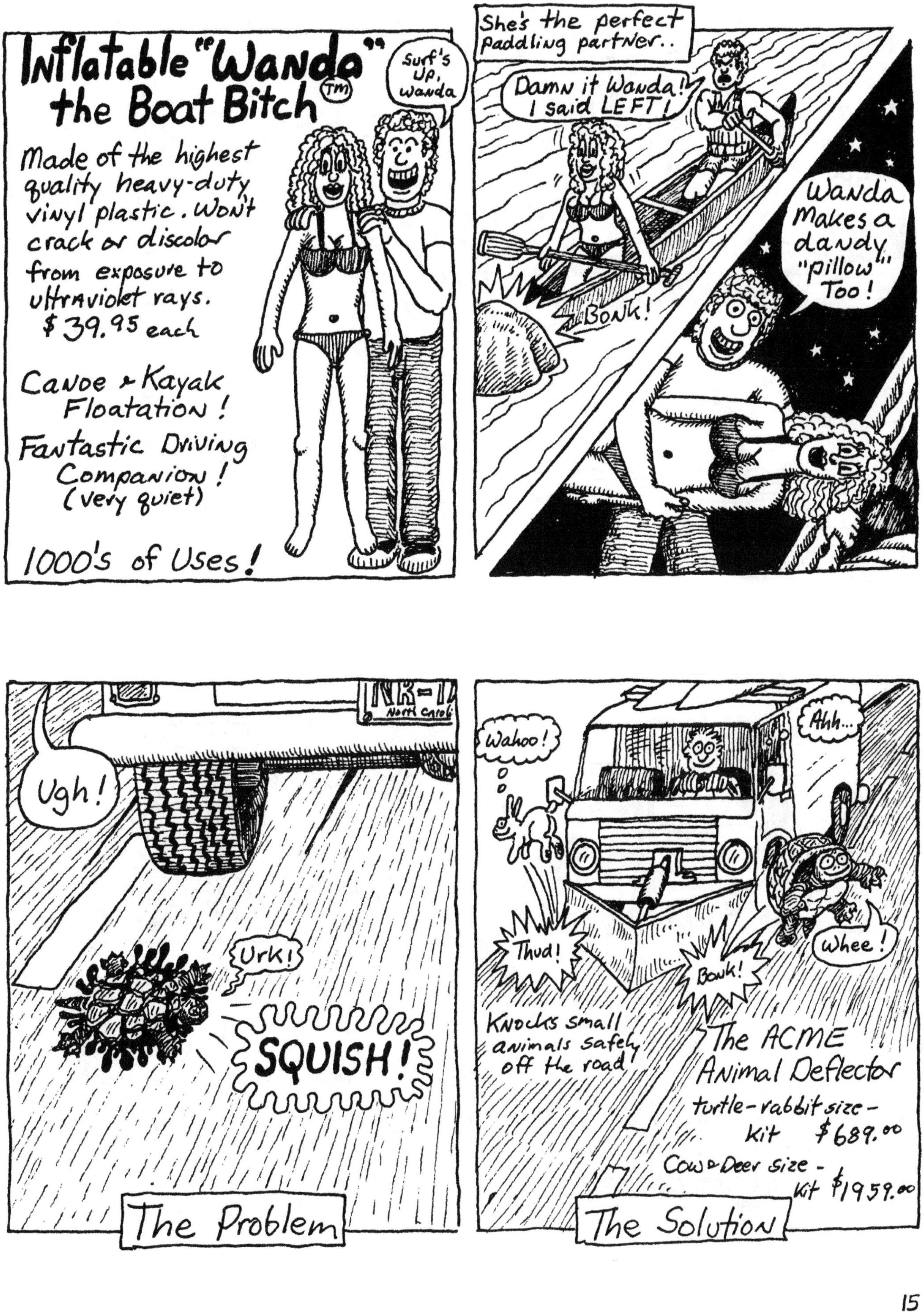
Inflatable "Wanda" the Boat Bitch (TM)
Surf's Up, wanda
Made of the highest quality heavy-duty vinyl plastic. Won't crack or discolor from exposure to ultraviolet rays. $39.95 each
Canoe & Kayak Floatation!
Fantastic Driving Companion! (very quiet)
1000's of Uses!
She's the perfect paddling partner..
Damn it Wanda! I said LEFT!
BONK!
Wanda Makes a dandy "pillow" Too!
Ugh!
Urk!
SQUISH!
The Problem
Wahoo!
Ahh...
Thud!
Bonk!
Whee!
Knocks small animals safely off the road
The ACME Animal Deflector
turtle-rabbit size - Kit $689.00
Cow & Deer size - Kit $1959.00
The Solution

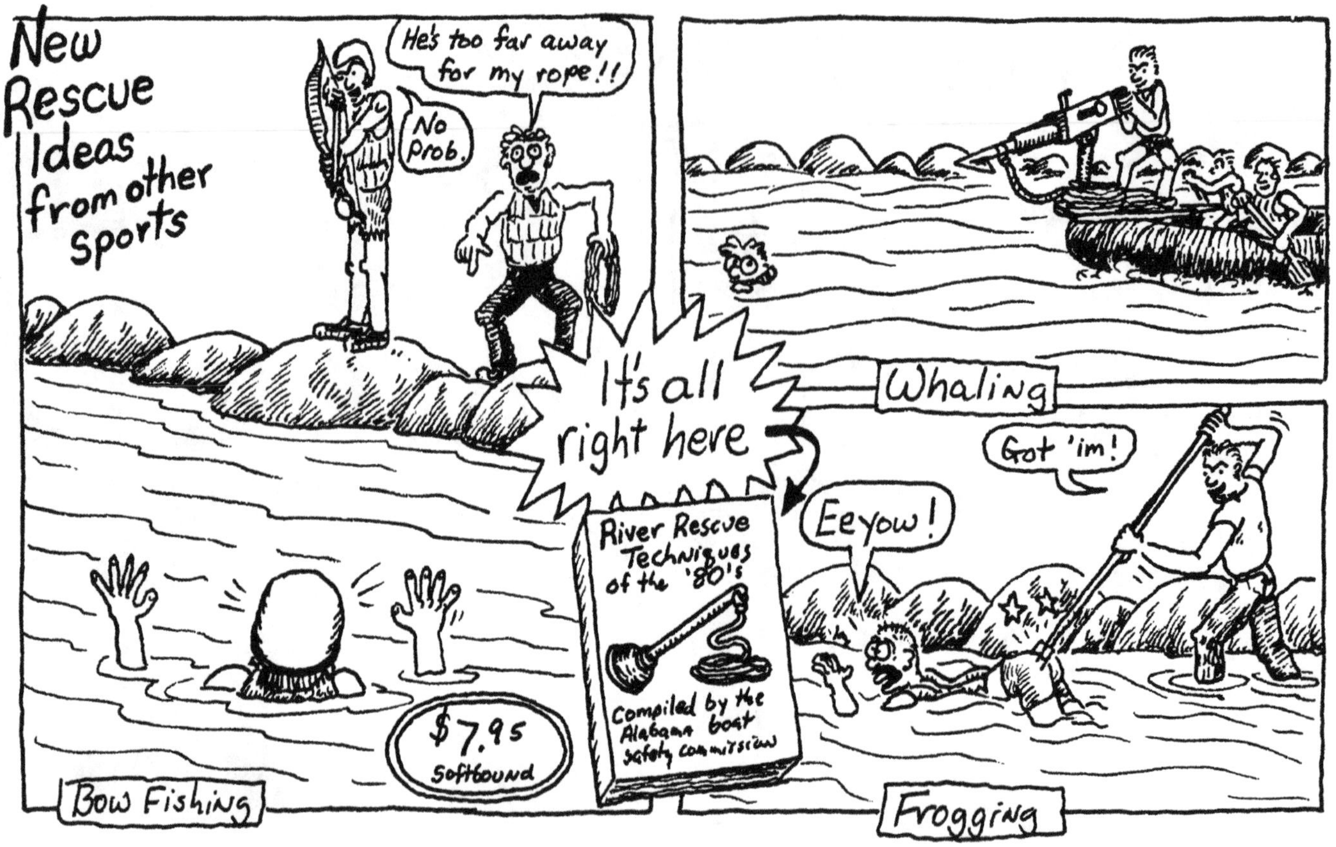
New Rescue Ideas from other Sports
He's too far away for my rope!!
No Prob.
Bow Fishing
It's all right here
River Rescue Techniques of the '80's
Compiled by the Alabama boat safety commission
$7.95 Softbound
Whaling
Got 'im!
Eeyow!
Frogging

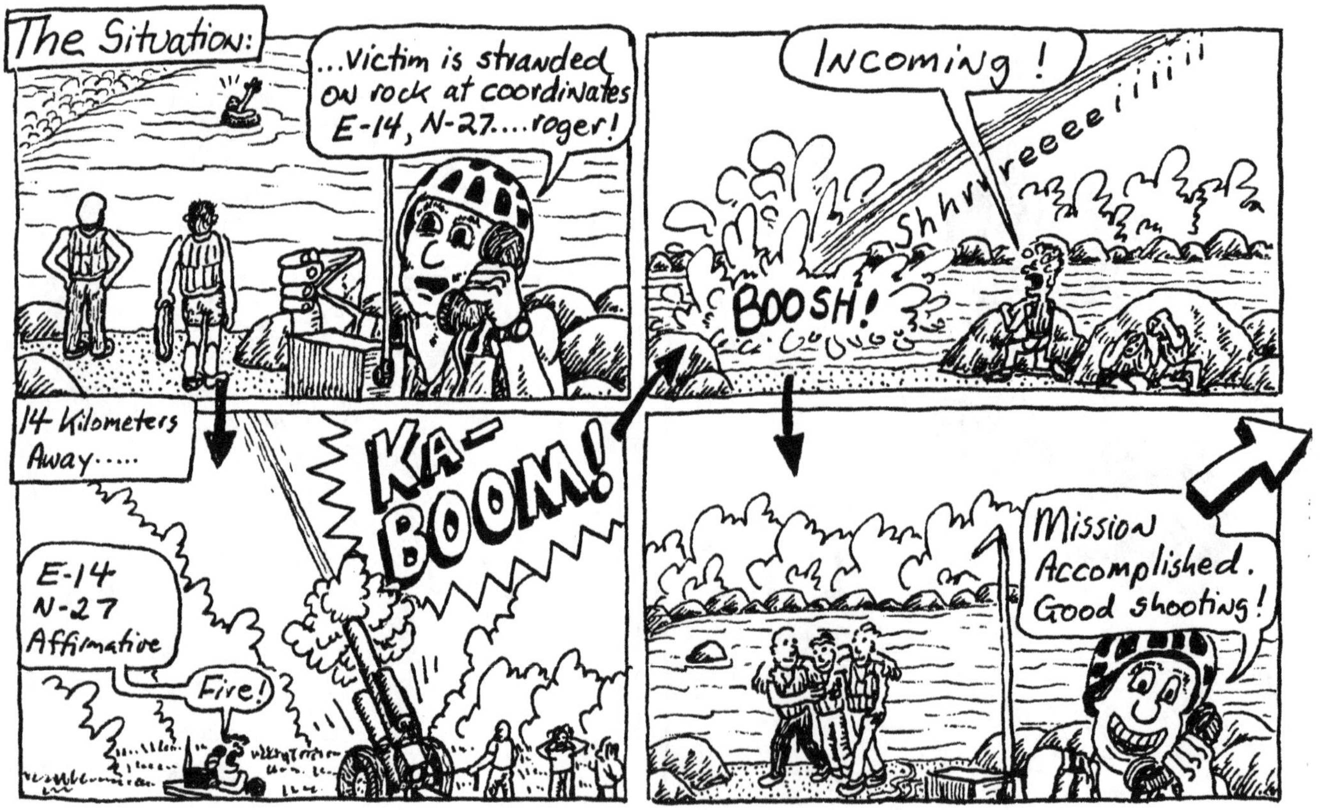
The Situation:
...victim is stranded on rock at coordinates E-14, N-27....roger!
14 Kilometers Away.....
E-14 N-27 Affimative
Fire!
KA-BOOM!
Incoming!
BOOSH!
Mission Accomplished. Good shooting!

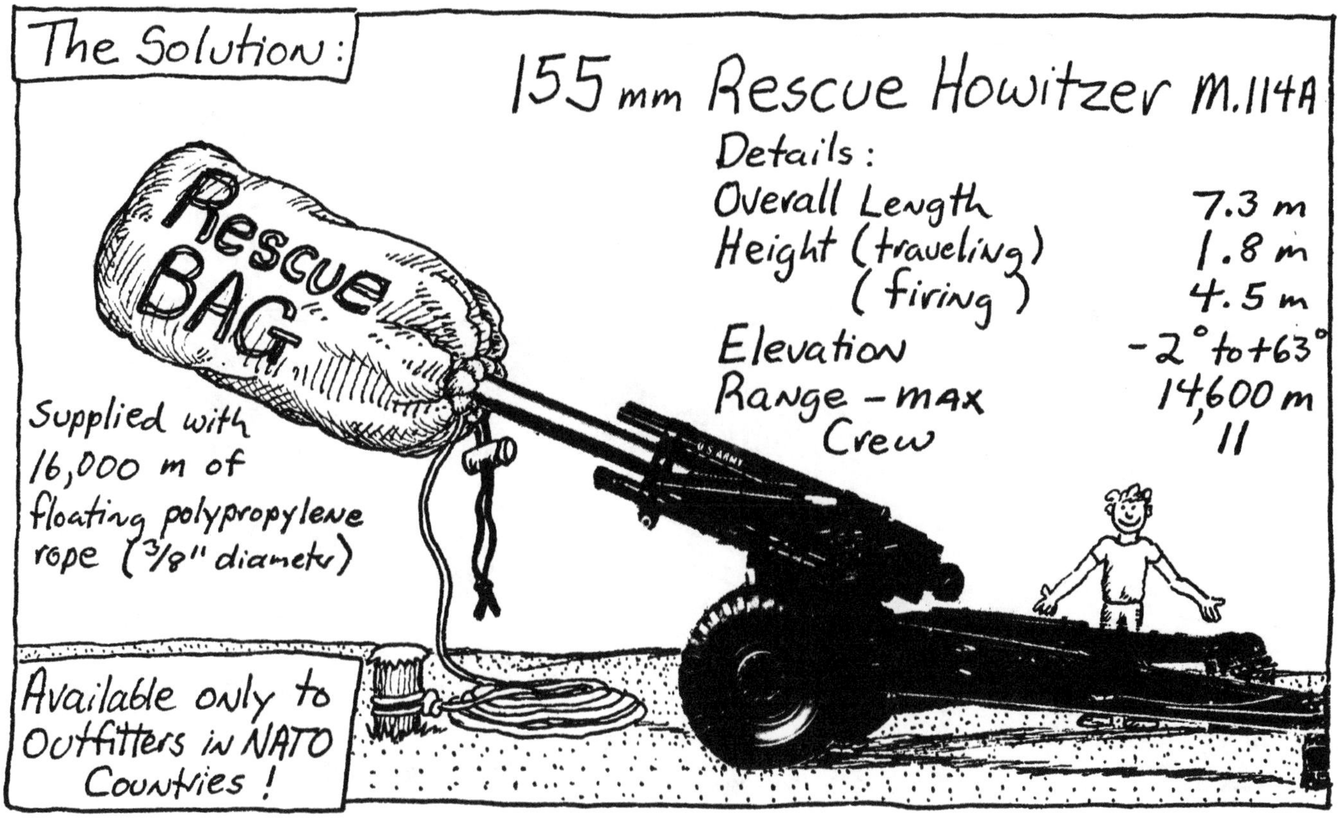
The Solution:
155 mm Rescue Howitzer M.114A
Details:
Overall Length 7.3 m
Height (traveling) 1.8 m
(firing) 4.5 m
Elevation -2° to +63°
Range - max 14,600 m
Crew 11
Rescue BAG
U.S. ARMY
Supplied with 16,000 m of floating polypropylene rope (3/8" diameter)
Available only to Outfitters in NATO Countries!

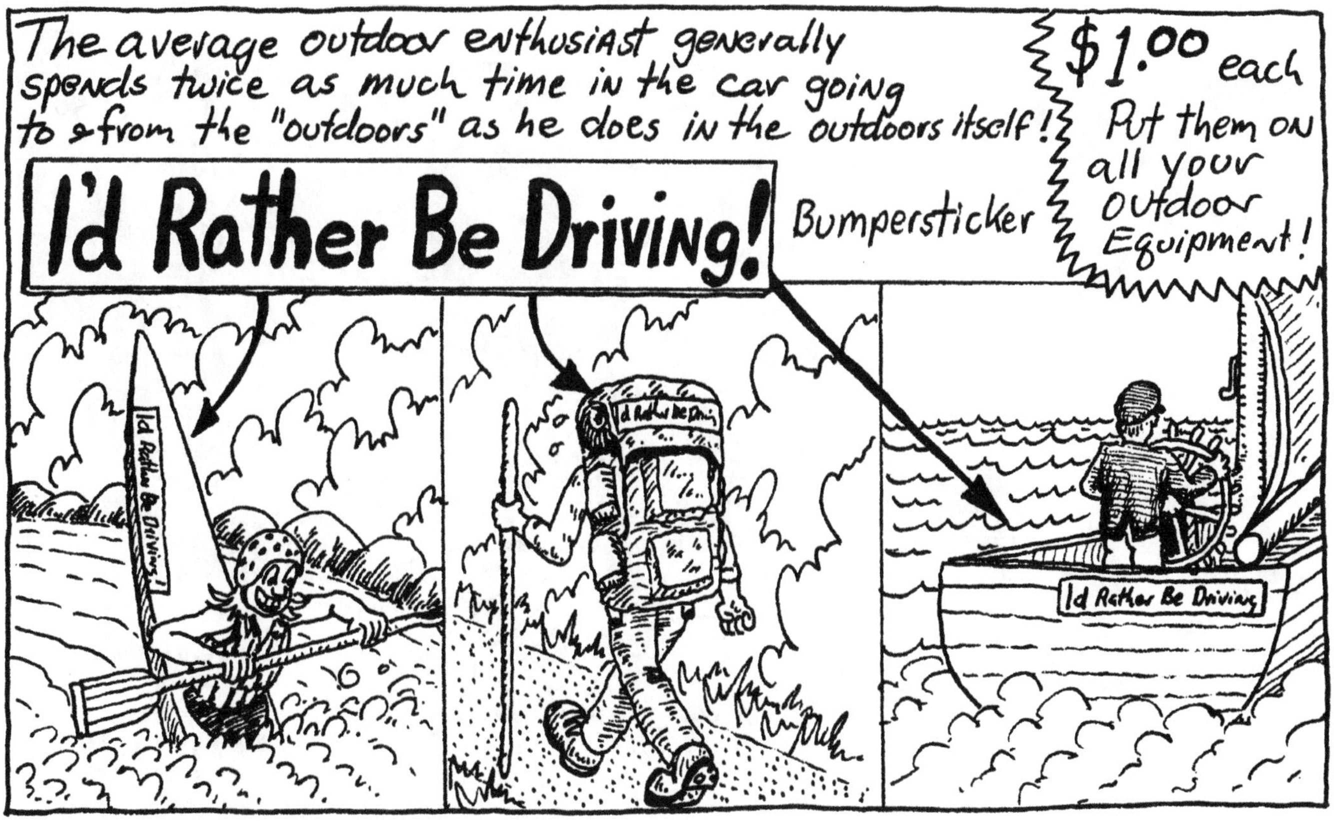
The average outdoor enthusiast generally spends twice as much time in the car going to & from the "outdoors" as he does in the outdoors itself!
$1.00 each
Put them on all your outdoor Equipment!
I'd Rather Be Driving!
Bumpersticker
Id Rather Be Driving!
Id Rather Be Driving

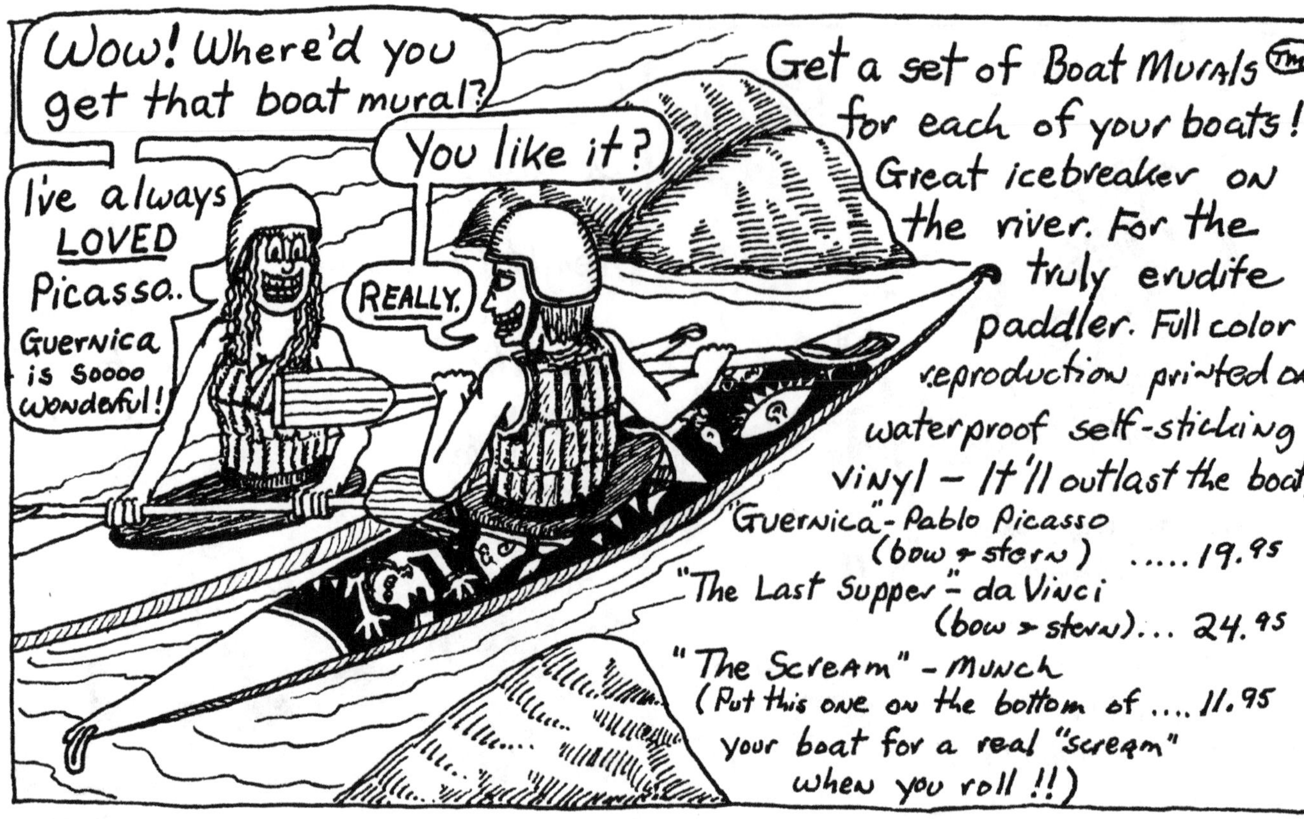
Wow! Where'd you get that boat mural?
I've always LOVED Picasso.. Guernica is soooo wonderful!
You like it?
REALLY.
Get a set of Boat Murals TM for each of your boats! Great icebreaker on the river. For the truly erudite paddler. Full color reproduction printed on waterproof self-sticking vinyl – It'll outlast the boat!
"Guernica" - Pablo Picasso (bow & stern) 19.95
"The Last Supper" - da Vinci (bow & stern)... 24.95
"The Scream" - Munch (Put this one on the bottom of .... 11.95 your boat for a real "scream" when you roll !!)

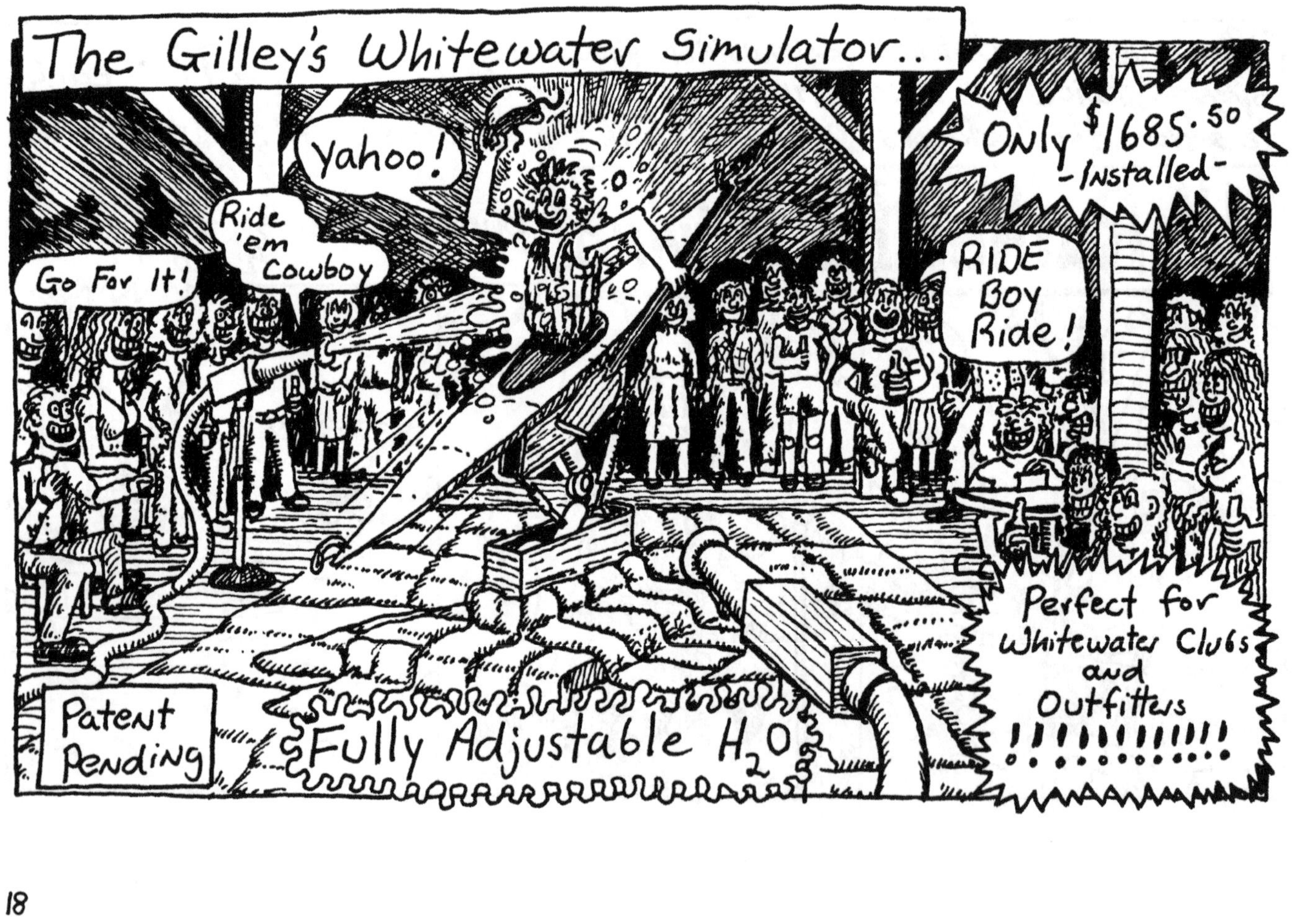
The Gilley's Whitewater Simulator...
Yahoo!
Ride 'em Cowboy
Go For It!
Only $1685.50 - Installed -
RIDE Boy Ride!
Perfect for Whitewater Clubs and Outfitters !!!!!!!!!!!!
Patent Pending
Fully Adjustable H2O

Over the last few years we at S&M River Tours have noticed a strange phenomenon... The very trips that the outfitter thinks will result in dissatisfied customers or (Heaven Forbid!) lawsuits are the very trips the customers loved best!

Broken legs, hypothermia, heat stroke, disease, Abusive or violent river guides, terrible weather, flooded rivers... They love it! They can't get enough of it! In response to overwhelming demand, S&M River Tours has put together some river trips for those customers who insist on a true wilderness ordeal!

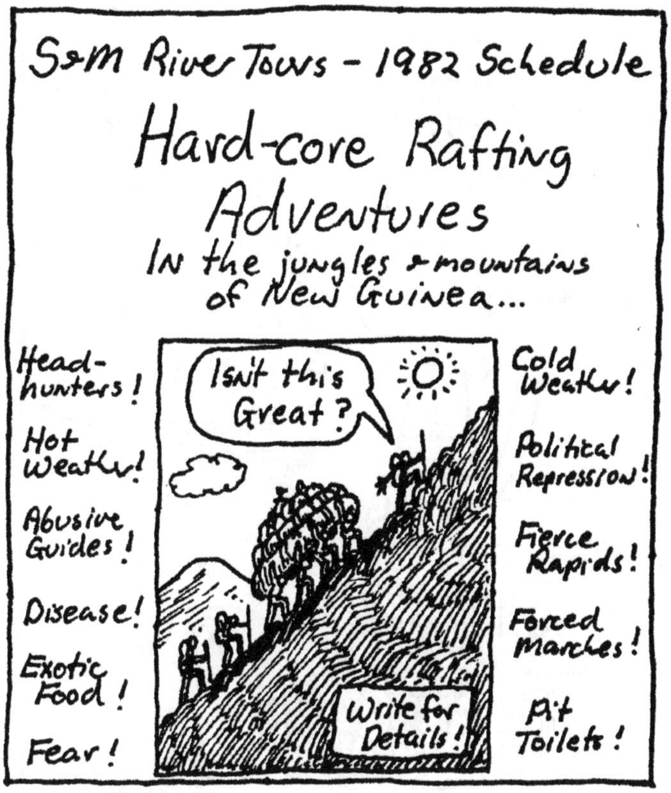
S&M River Tours - 1982 Schedule
Hard-core Rafting Adventures
In the jungles & mountains of New Guinea...
Head-hunters!
Hot Weather!
Abusive Guides!
Disease!
Exotic Food!
Fear!
Isn't this Great?
Write for Details!
Cold Weather!
Political Repression!
Fierce Rapids!
Forced Marches!
Pit Toilets!

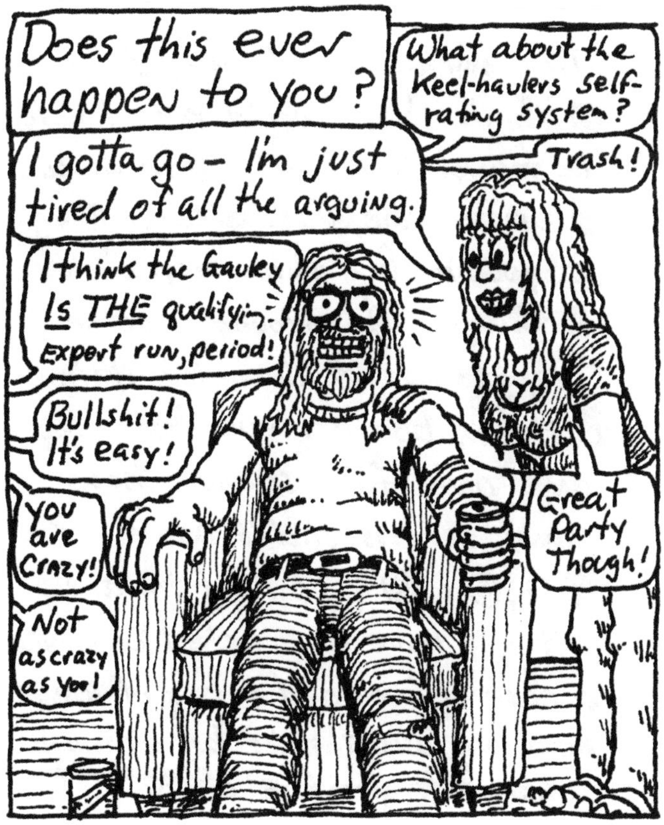
Does this ever happen to you?
What about the Keel-haulers self-rating system?
Trash!
I gotta go - I'm just tired of all the arguing.
I think the Gauley IS THE qualifying expert run, period!
Bullshit! It's easy!
You are Crazy!
Not as crazy as you!
Great Party Though!

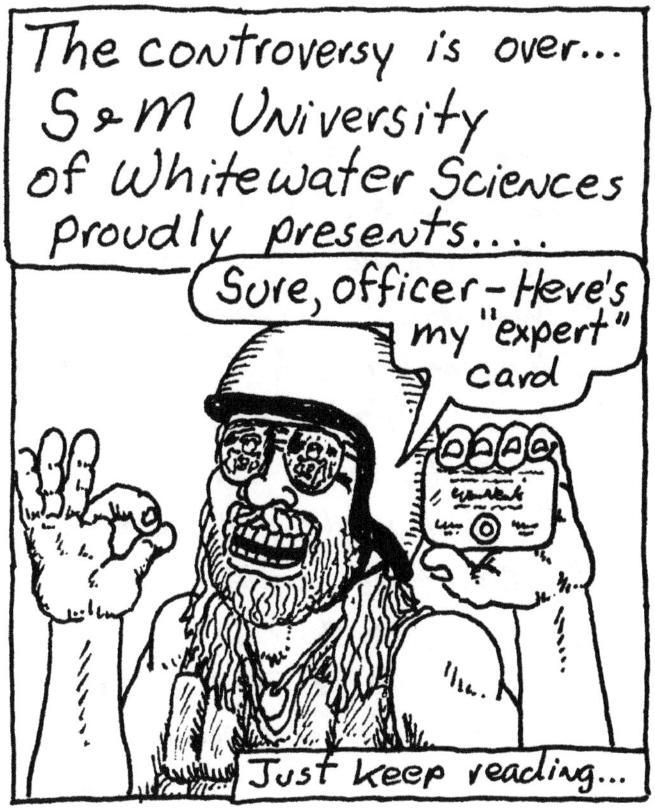
The controversy is over... S&M University of Whitewater Sciences proudly presents....
Sure, officer - Here's my "expert" card
Just keep reading...

Turn this...
But officer! The "River Closed" signs must have been under water or washed away......
Shut up, kid! Git in the squad car.
Into this.
Yes sir! We'll be sure to make sure everybody on the river has an expert card!
With This!

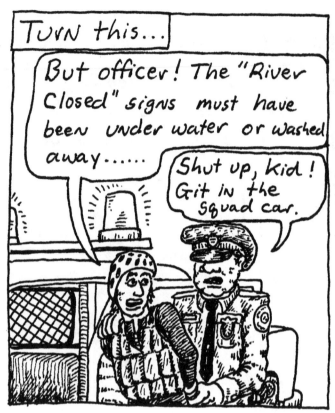

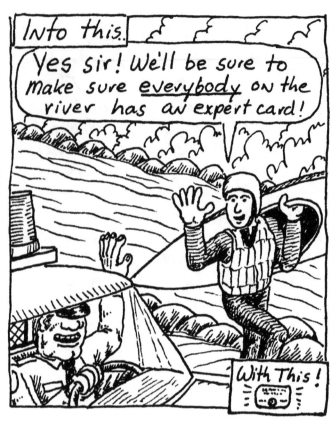

Examination for Whitewater Doctorate-

1. Things you can surf: Ⓐ Rock, Ⓑ Tree Ⓒ Wave, Ⓓ Cat
2. The correct spelling of "Nantahala" is: Ⓐ "Nantehila" Ⓑ "Nontahula" Ⓒ "Nantahala" Ⓓ "Nannyheela"
3. [Fill in the blank] A kayak paddle has ____ blades- Ⓐ three Ⓑ one Ⓒ two Ⓓ large curved...
4. The distinguishing characteristic of a Class three rapid is: Ⓐ Trees Ⓑ Anaphylactic Shock Ⓒ maneuvering is necessary Ⓓ The Treaty of Ghent
5. "It is impossible for a person of the female persuasion to roll a kayak." True or False (circle one) T F
6. Thigh straps would most likely be found in a (an)... Ⓐ frying pan, Ⓑ hamster cage, Ⓒ decked canoe, Ⓓ egg
7. Synonym for "throw rope"- Ⓐ thingie Ⓑ Compound fracture, Ⓒ rapid floss Ⓓ Alexander Haig
8. If six boaters run Iron Ring and only four survive, how many boaters didn't make it? Ⓐ 0, Ⓑ 1, Ⓒ 2, Ⓓ All of the above
9. If you have an ice chest containing a case of beer and a bag of ice, how long will the ice last with an ambient temperature of 90°F.?

(A) 1 hour (B) 6 hours (C) It doesn't make any difference (D) 8 hours

(10) Which of the following was not a famous whitewater boater? (A) Walt Blackadar (B) John Wesley Powell (C) Truman Capote (D) William Nealy

(11) Calculate the chances of a successful inner tube run on the Gauley at 4,500 c.f.s. - (A) 50% (B) 10% (C) 0% (D) 80%

(12) Means the front of the boat. (A) snout (B) bumper (C) bow (D) dingus

Stop!

Correct Answers - (1) c, (2) c, (3) c, (4) c, (5) False (stupid!), (6) c, (7) c, (8) c, (9) c, (10) c, (11) c, (12) c

If you answered more than 60% of the questions correctly, you are now an Expert Boater. Raise your right hand and state; "I never come out of my boat!"

Congratulations!

You may sign your card.

Tiny black frames Available!

cut along dotted line

S&M University of Whitewater Sciences
Chapel Hill, North Carolina

Know All men By These Presents That Upon This Date, S&M University Has Conferred Upon

---

the Degree of
Doctor of Whitewater Science

W. Nealy
Dean of the College

S&M UNIVERSITY E Pluribus Unum 1982

William Nealy
President

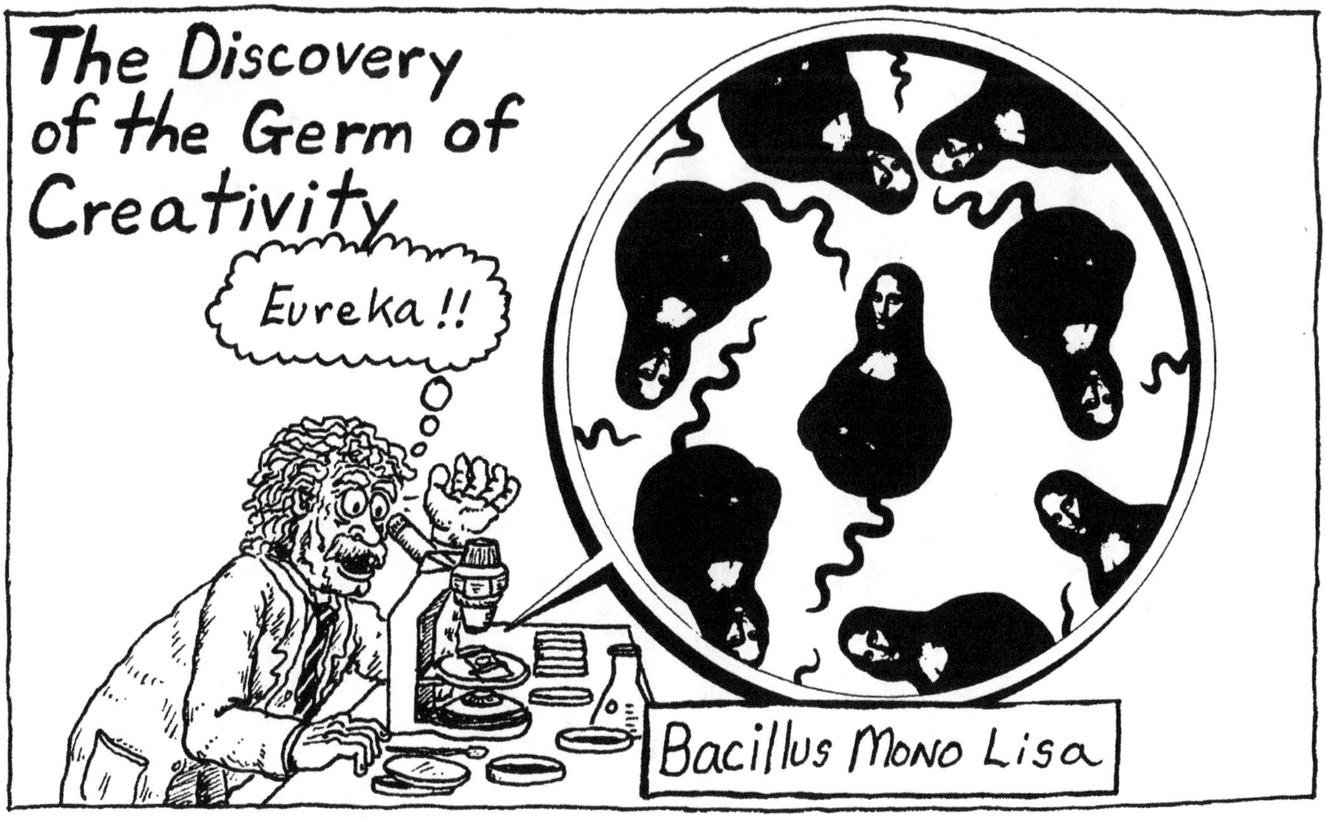

The Discovery of the Germ of Creativity
Eureka!!
Bacillus Mono Lisa

Another Paddling Trip....

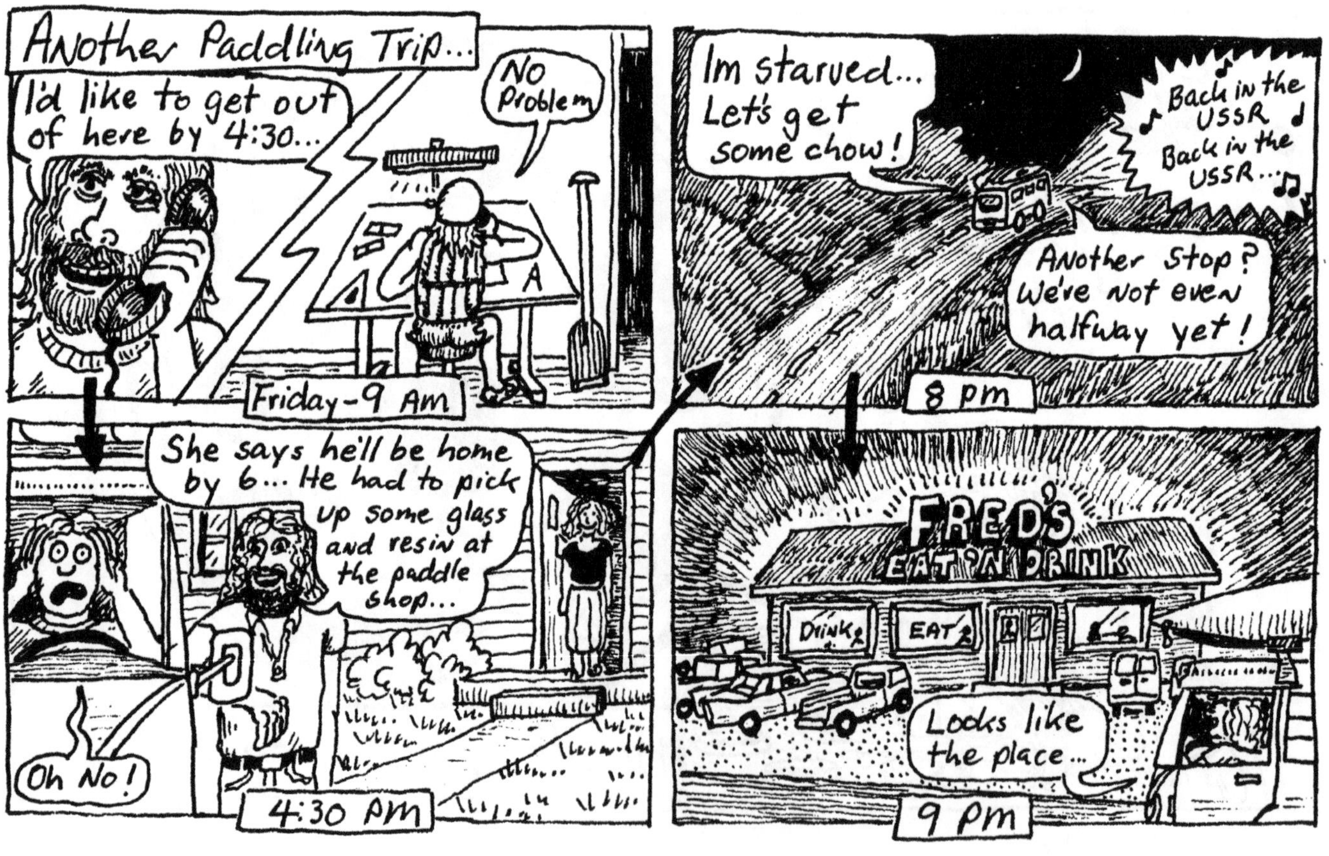
Another Paddling Trip...
I'd like to get out of here by 4:30...
No Problem
Friday-9 AM
She says he'll be home by 6... He had to pick up some glass and resin at the paddle shop...
Oh No!
4:30 PM
Im starved... Let's get some chow!
Back in the USSR Back in the USSR...
Another Stop? We're not even halfway yet!
8 pm
FRED'S
EAT 'N DRINK
DRINK
EAT
Looks like the place...
9 pm

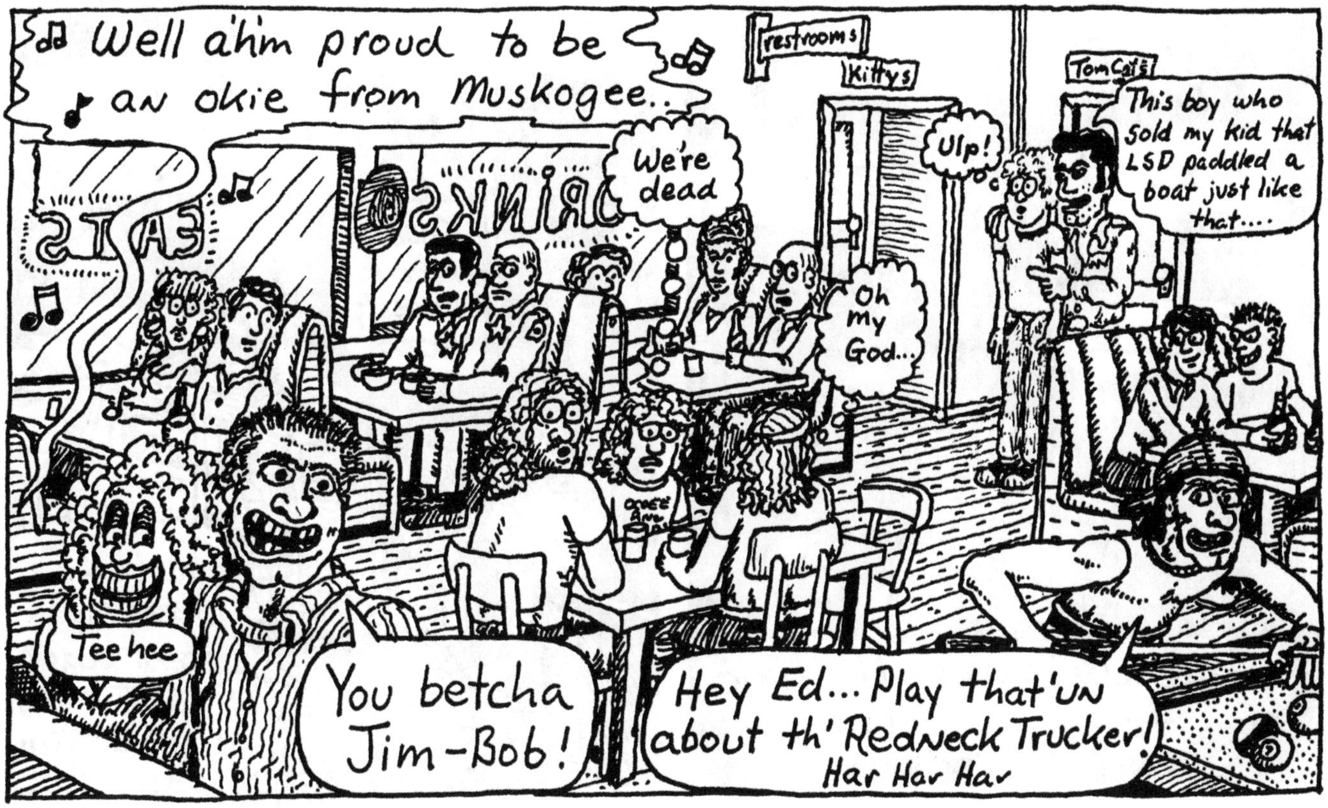
Well a'him proud to be an okie from Muskogee..
restrooms
Kittys
Tom Cats
EATS
DRINKS
We're dead
Ulp!
This boy who sold my kid that LSD paddled a boat just like that....
Oh my God...
Tee hee
You betcha Jim-Bob!
Hey Ed... Play that'un about th' Redneck Trucker!
Har Har Har

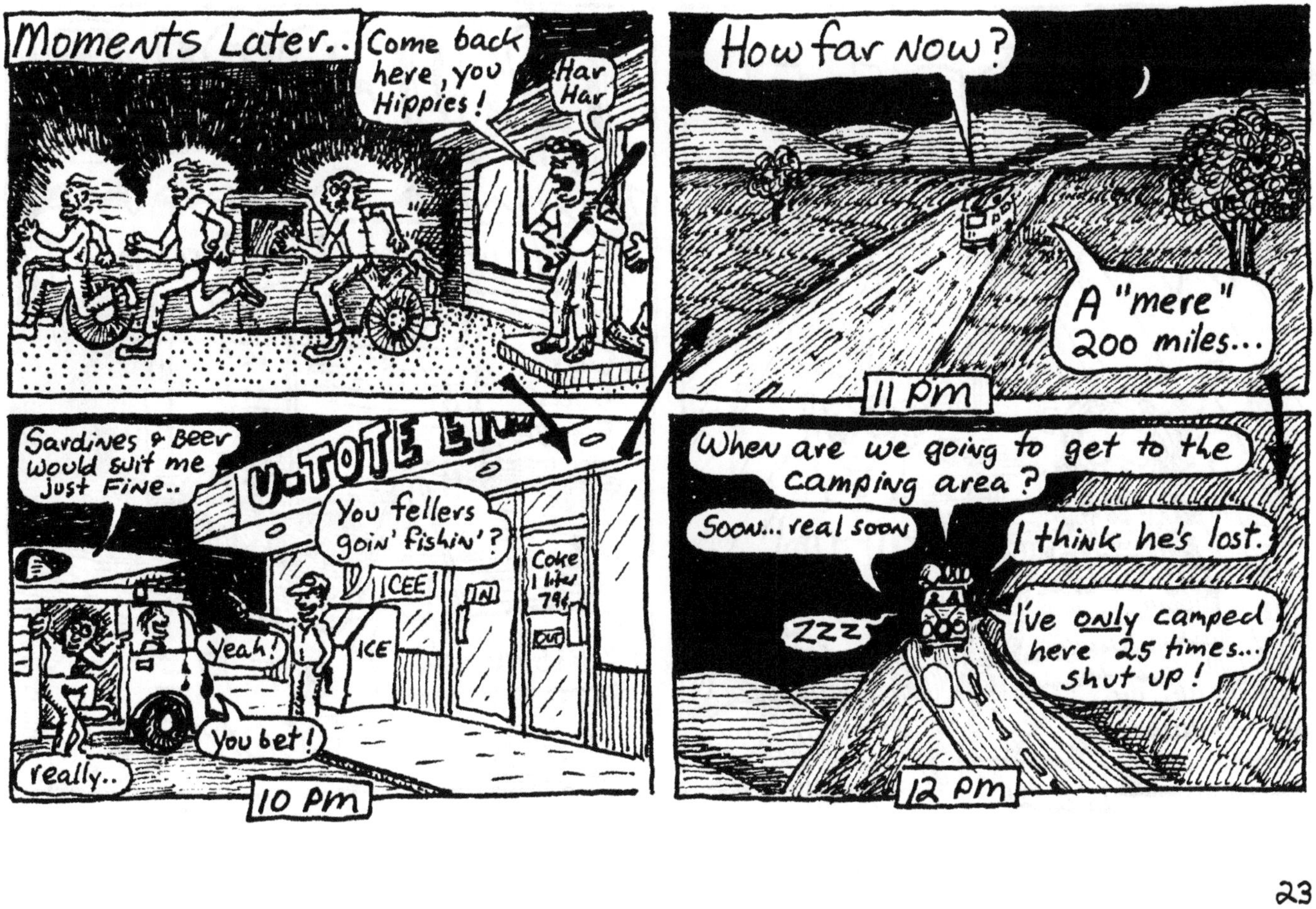
Moments Later..
Come back here, you Hippies!
Har Har
How far now?
A "mere" 200 miles...
11 PM
Sardines & Beer would suit me just Fine..
U-TOTE EM
You fellers goin' fishin'?
Coke 1 liter 79¢
ICEE
IN
OUT
ICE
Yeah!
You bet!
really..
10 PM
When are we going to get to the camping area?
Soon... real soon
I think he's lost.
ZZZ
I've only camped here 25 times... shut up!
12 PM

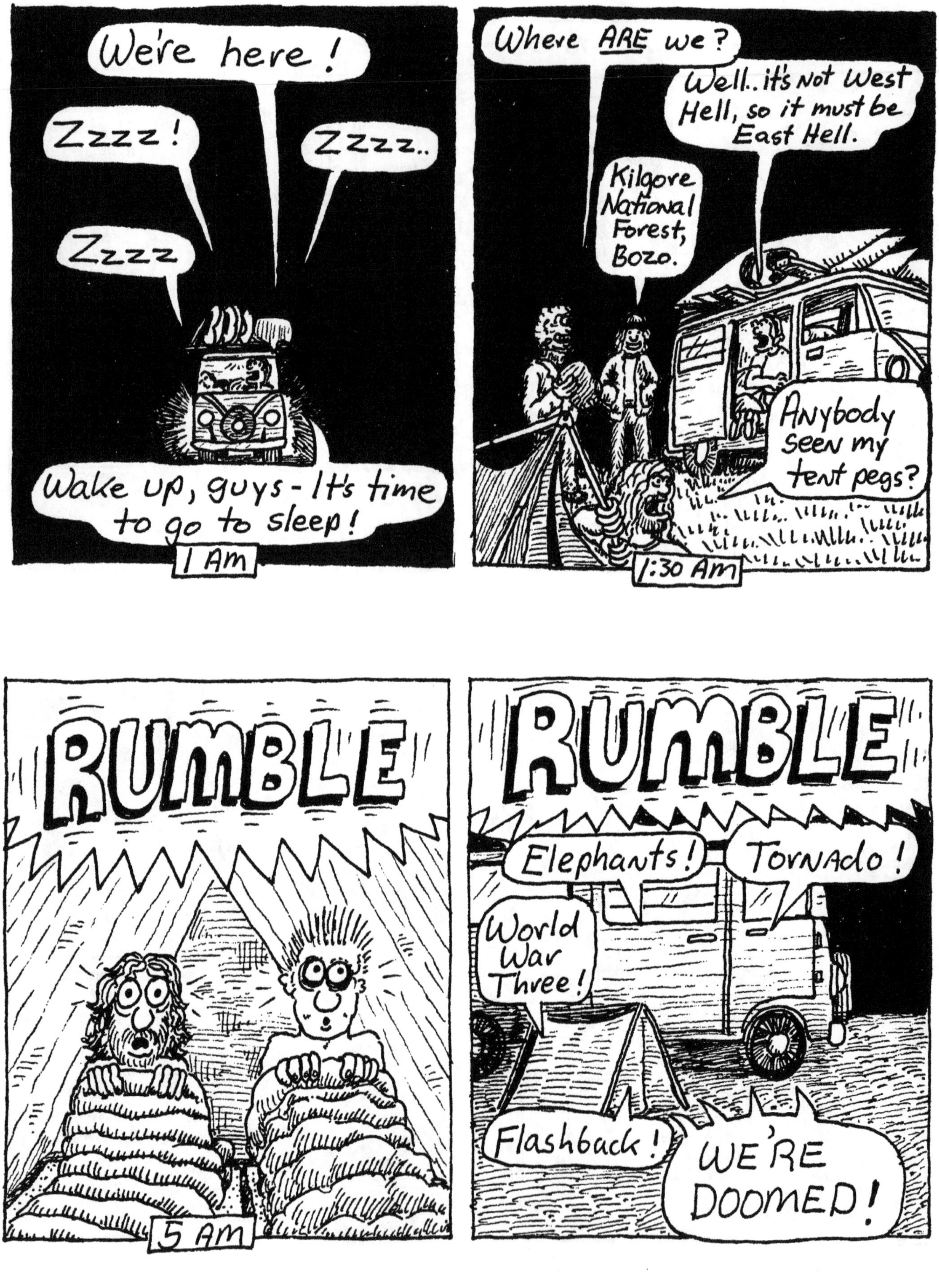
We're here!
Zzzz!
Zzzz..
Zzzz
Wake up, guys - It's time to go to sleep!
1 AM
Where ARE we?
Well.. it's not West Hell, so it must be East Hell.
Kilgore National Forest, Bozo.
Anybody seen my tent pegs?
1:30 AM
RUMBLE
5 AM
RUMBLE
Elephants!
Tornado!
World War Three!
Flashback!
WE'RE DOOMED!

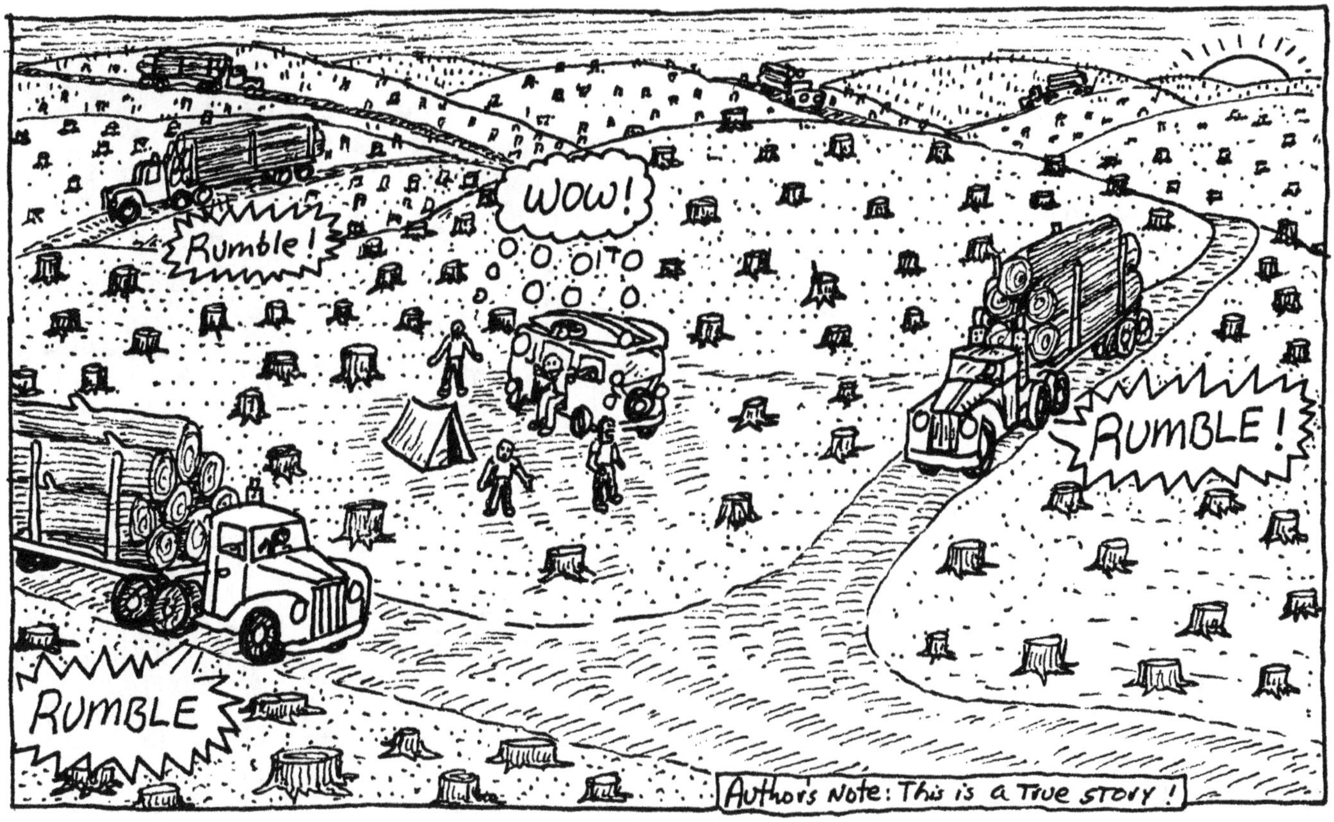
WOW!
Rumble!
RUMBLE!
RUMBLE
Author's Note: This is a True STORY!

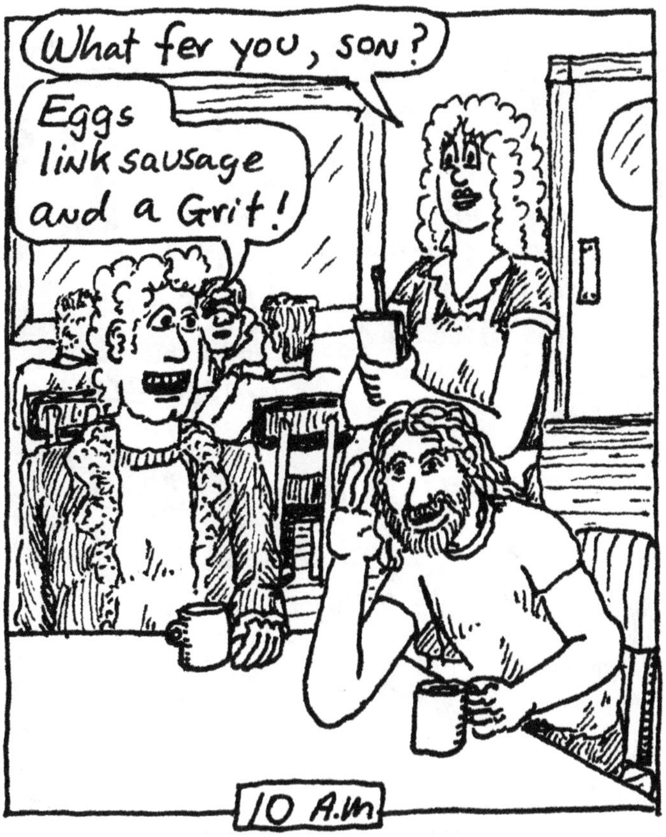
What fer you, son?
Eggs link sausage and a Grit!
10 A.M.

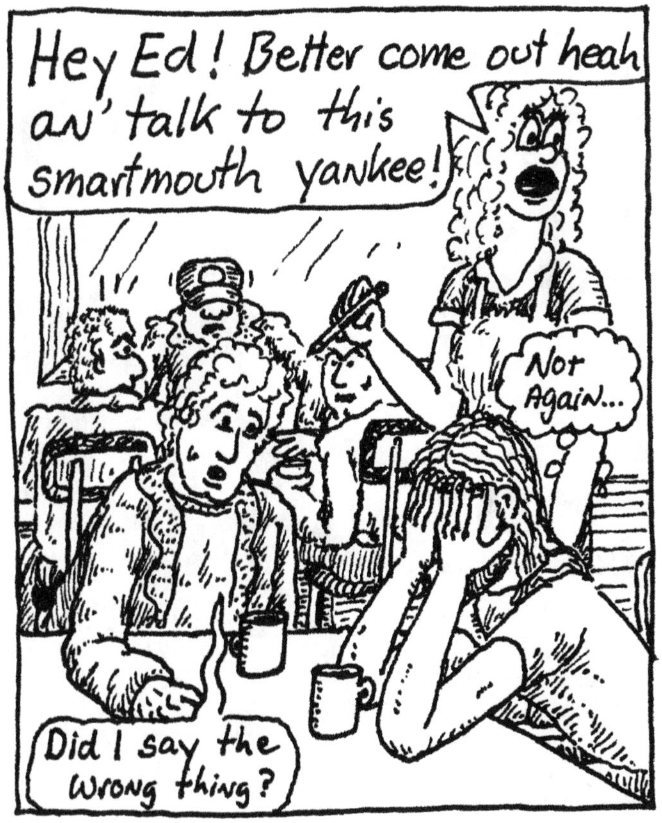
Hey Ed! Better come out heah an' talk to this smartmouth yankee!
Not Again...
Did I say the wrong thing?

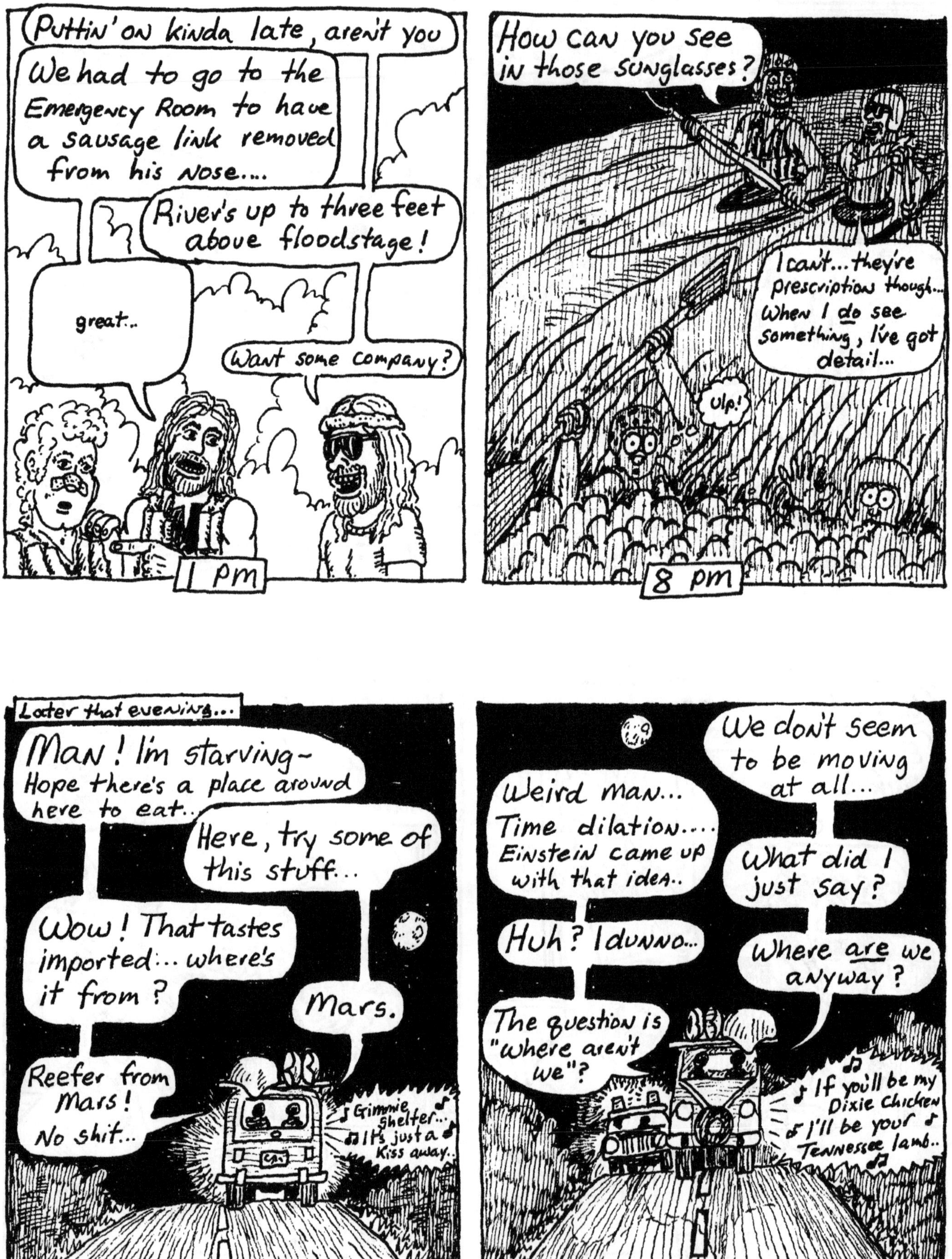
Puttin' on kinda late, aren't you
We had to go to the Emergency Room to have a sausage link removed from his nose....
River's up to three feet above floodstage!
great..
Want some company?
1 pm
How can you see in those sunglasses?
I can't... they're prescription though... When I do see something, I've got detail...
Ulp!
8 pm
Later that evening...
Man! I'm starving- Hope there's a place around here to eat..
Here, try some of this stuff...
Wow! That tastes imported... where's it from?
Mars.
Reefer from Mars! No shit...
Gimmie shelter... It's just a kiss away..
We don't seem to be moving at all...
Weird man... Time dilation.... Einstein came up with that idea..
What did I just say?
Huh? I dunno...
Where are we anyway?
The question is "where aren't we"?
If you'll be my Dixie Chicken I'll be your Tennessee lamb..

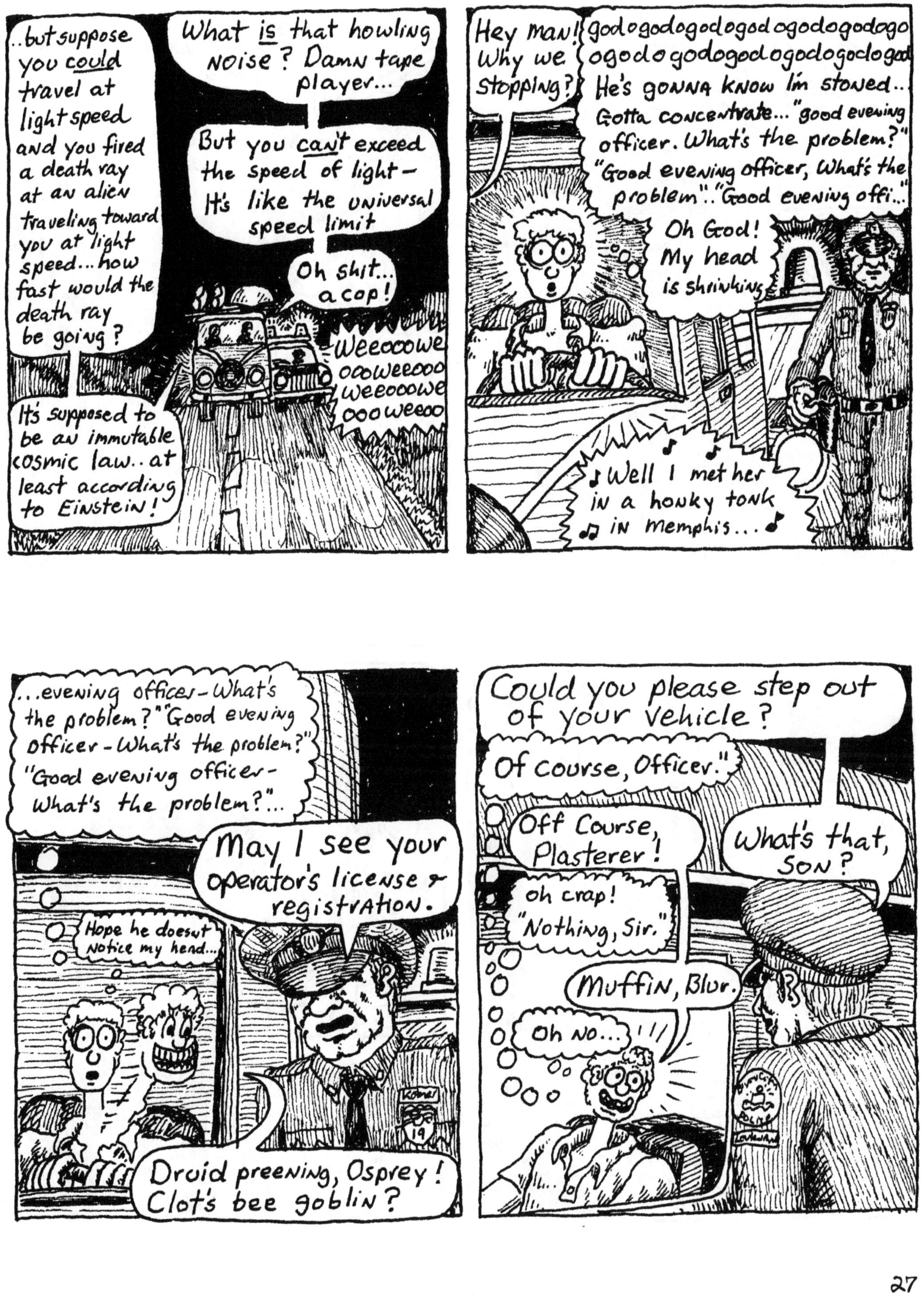
..but suppose you could travel at light speed and you fired a death ray at an alien traveling toward you at light speed... how fast would the death ray be going?
What is that howling noise? Damn tape player...
But you can't exceed the speed of light— It's like the universal speed limit
It's supposed to be an immutable cosmic law.. at least according to Einstein!
Oh shit... a cop!
Weeooowe oooweeooo weeooowe oooweeoo
Hey man! Why we stopping?
godogodogodogodogodogodogo ogodogodogodogodogodogod He's gonna know I'm stoned.. Gotta concentrate... "good evening officer. What's the problem?" "Good evening officer, What's the problem".."Good evening offi.."
Oh God! My head is shrinking
Well I met her in a honky tonk in memphis...
...evening officer—What's the problem?" "Good evening officer—What's the problem?" "Good evening officer—What's the problem?"...
May I see your operator's license & registration.
Hope he doesnt notice my head...
Druid preening, Osprey! Clot's bee goblin?
Could you please step out of your vehicle?
Of course, Officer."
Off Course, Plasterer!
What's that, son?
oh crap! "Nothing, Sir."
Muffin, Blur.
Oh no...

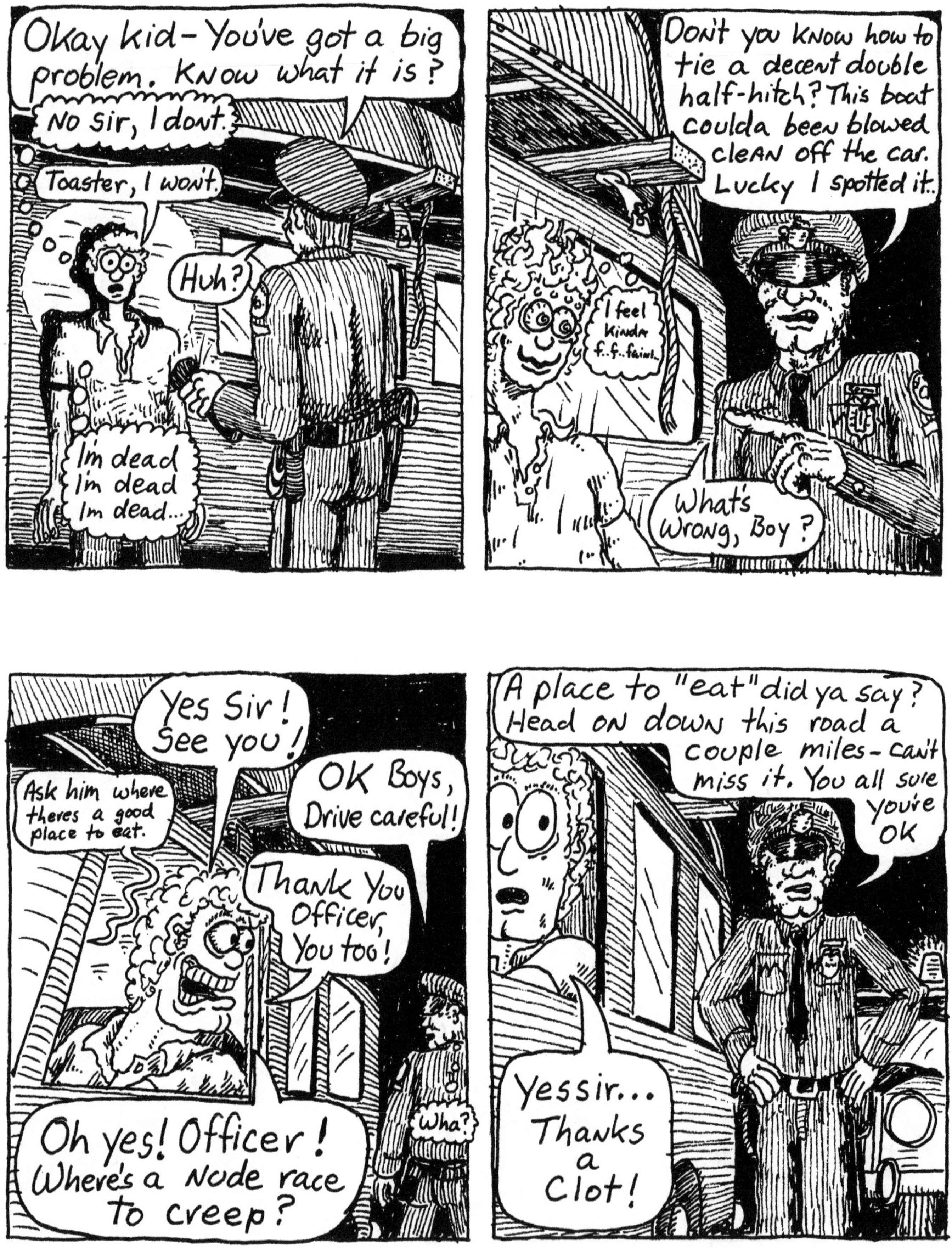
Okay kid- You've got a big problem. Know what it is?
No sir, I dont.
Toaster, I wont.
Huh?
I'm dead I'm dead Im dead...
Don't you know how to tie a decent double half-hitch? This boat coulda been blowed clean off the car. Lucky I spotted it.
I feel kinda f..f..faint.
What's wrong, Boy?
Ask him where theres a good place to eat.
Yes Sir! See you!
OK Boys, Drive careful!
Thank You Officer, You too!
Oh yes! Officer! Where's a node race to creep?
Wha?
A place to "eat" did ya say? Head on down this road a couple miles- can't miss it. You all sure you're OK
Yessir... Thanks a Clot!

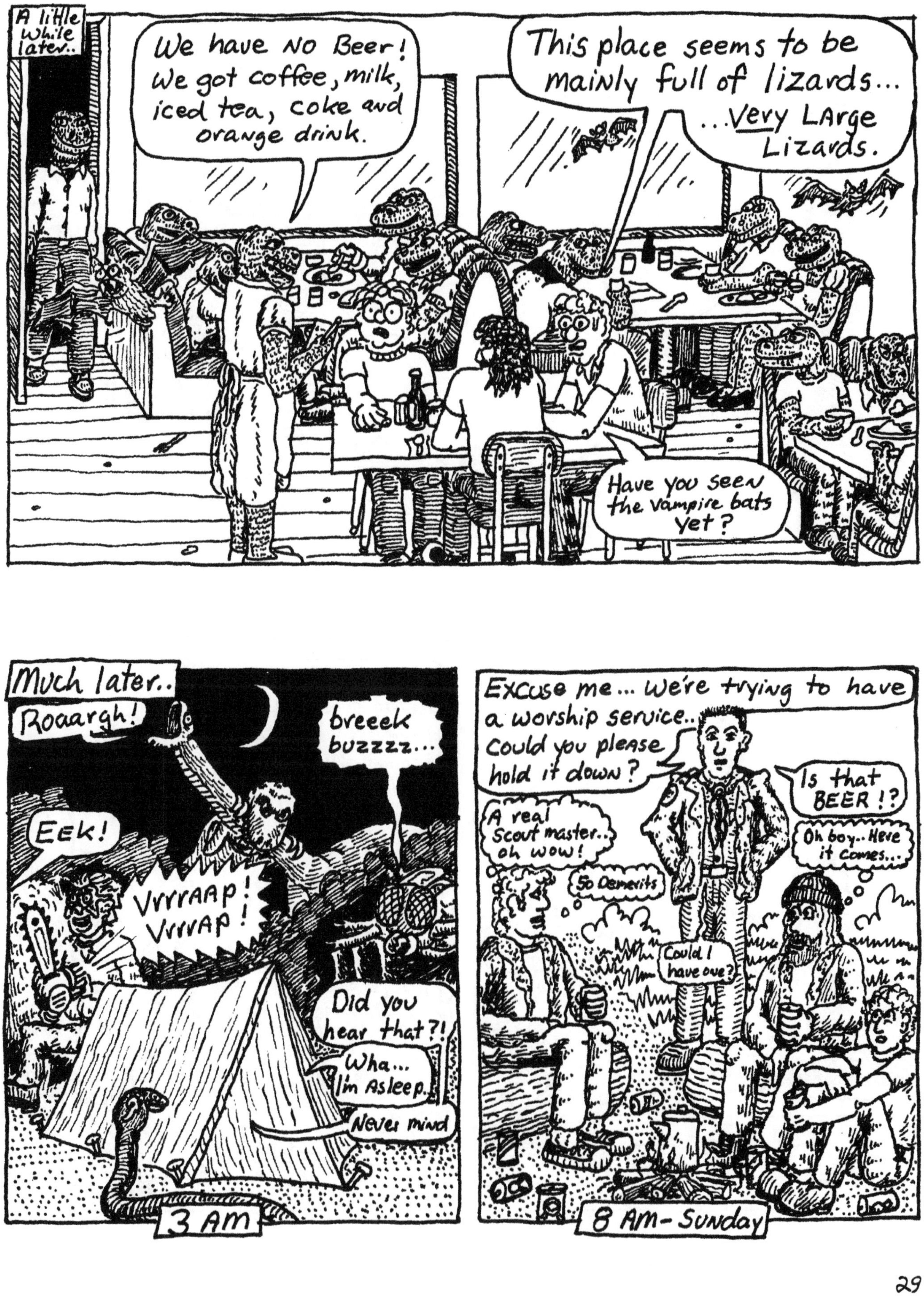
A little while later..
We have NO Beer! We got coffee, milk, iced tea, coke and orange drink.
This place seems to be mainly full of lizards...
...Very LArge Lizards.
Have you seen the vampire bats yet?
Much later..
Roaargh!
breeek buzzzz...
Eek!
Vrrraap! Vrrvap!
Did you hear that?!
Wha... I'm Asleep..
Never mind
3 AM
Excuse me... we're trying to have a worship service.. Could you please hold it down?
Is that BEER!?
A real Scout master.. oh wow!
Oh boy.. Here it comes...
50 Demerits
Could I have one?
8 AM-Sunday

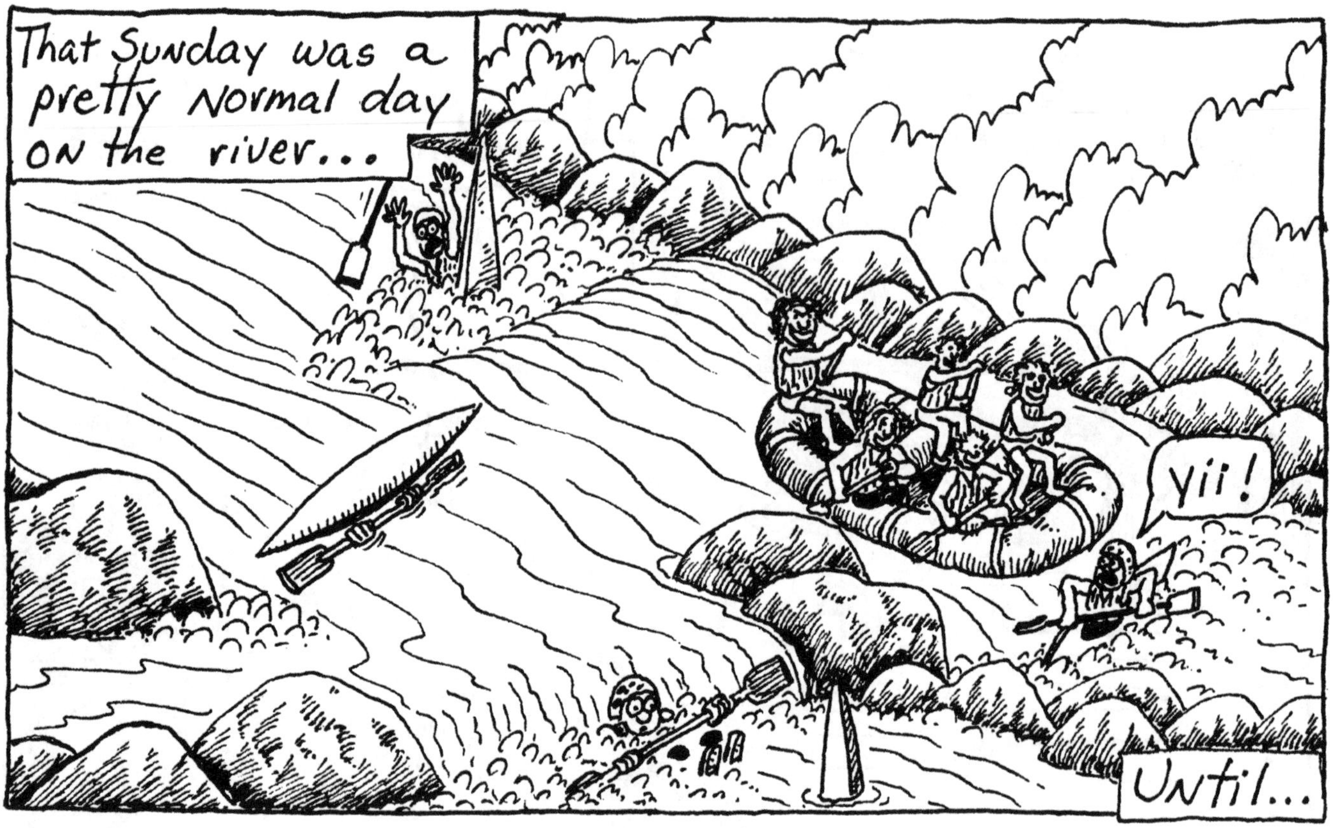
That Sunday was a pretty Normal day on the river...
yii!
Until...

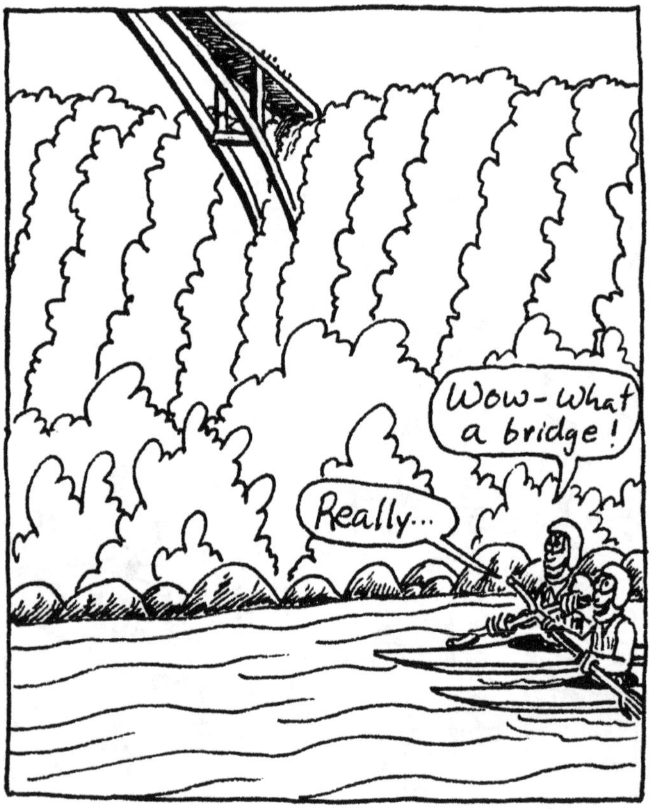
Wow-What a bridge!
Really...

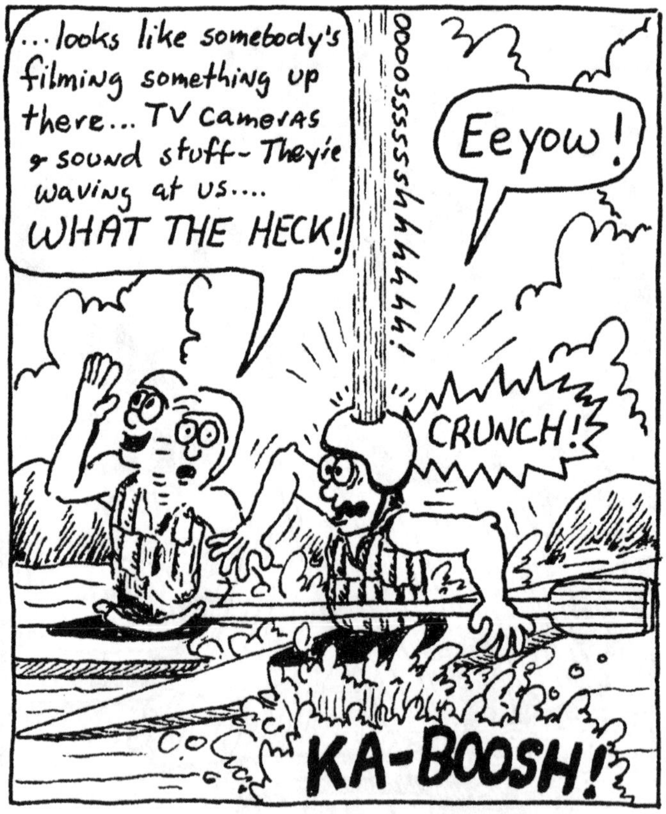
...looks like somebody's filming something up there... TV cameras & sound stuff- They're waving at us.... WHAT THE HECK!
Eeyow!
CRUNCH!
KA-BOOSH!

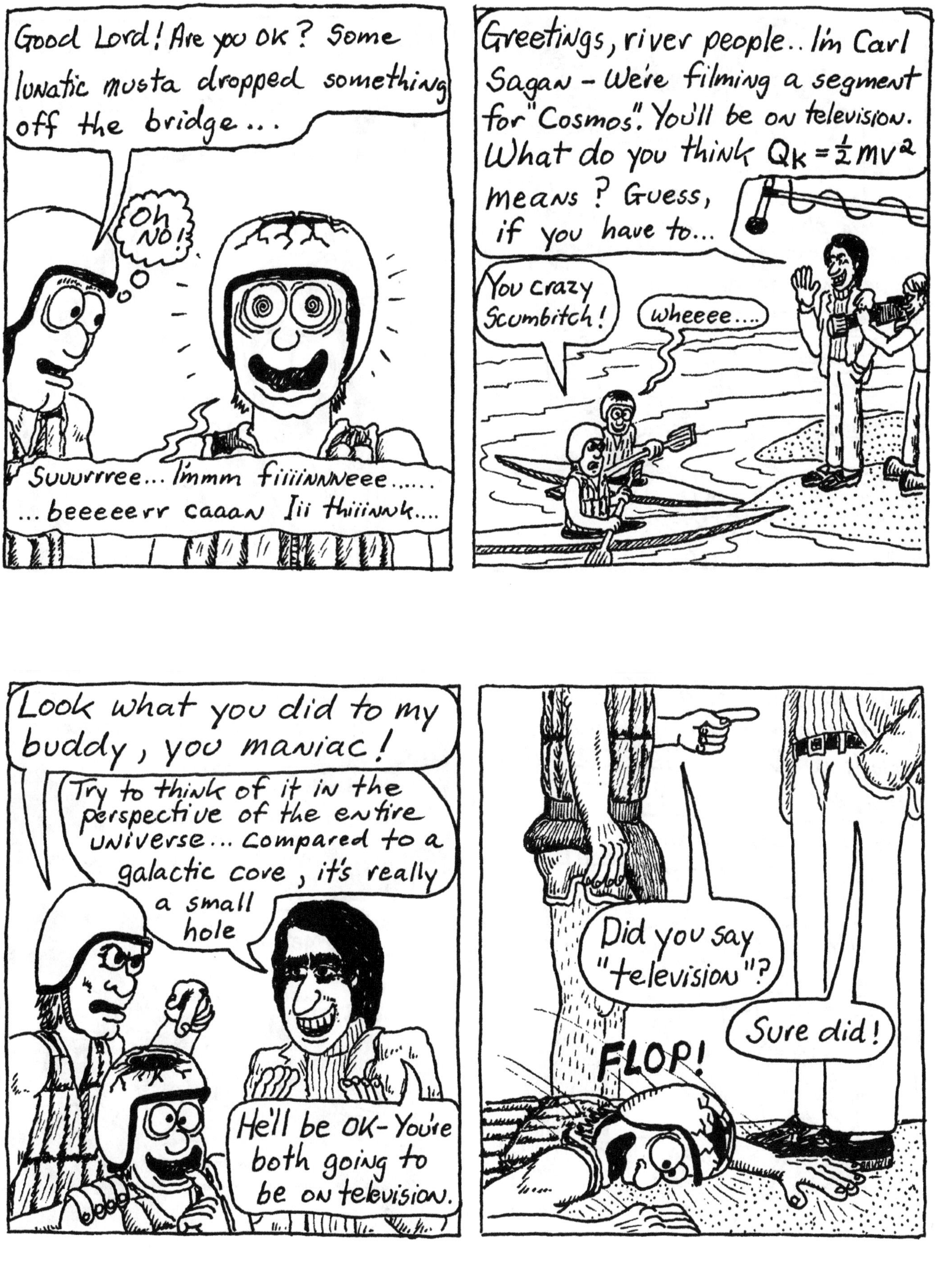
Good Lord! Are you OK? Some lunatic musta dropped something off the bridge...
Oh NO!
Suuurrree... Immm fiiiinnneee..... ...beeeeerr caaan Iii thiiinnk....
Greetings, river people.. I'm Carl Sagan - We're filming a segment for "Cosmos". You'll be on television. What do you think $Q_K = \frac{1}{2}mv^2$ means? Guess, if you have to...
You crazy Scumbitch!
wheeee....
Look what you did to my buddy, you maniac!
Try to think of it in the perspective of the entire universe... Compared to a galactic core, it's really a small hole
He'll be OK- You're both going to be on television.
Did you say "television"?
Sure did!
FLOP!

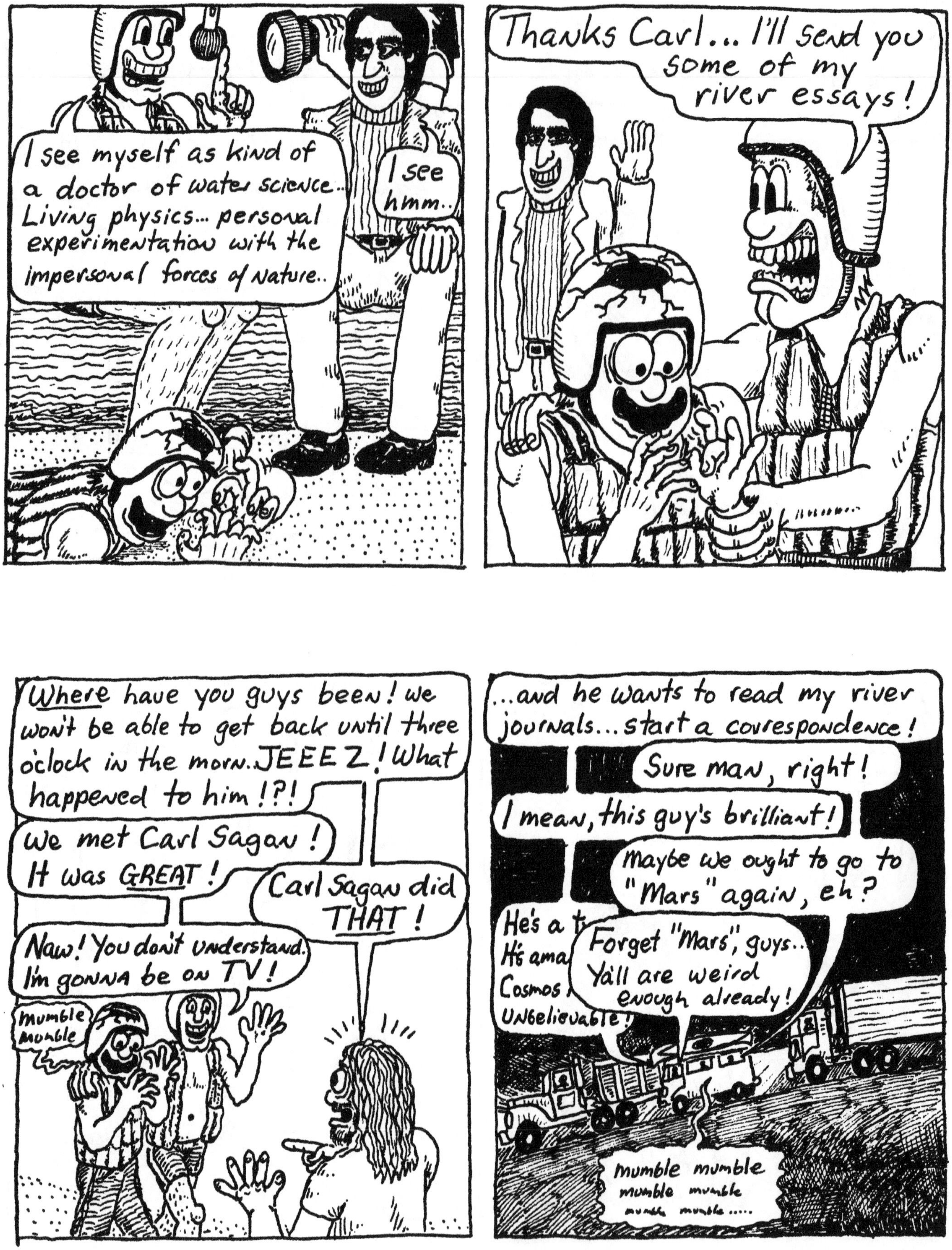
I see myself as kind of a doctor of water science.. Living physics... personal experimentation with the impersonal forces of Nature..
I see hmm..
Thanks Carl... I'll send you some of my river essays!
Where have you guys been! We won't be able to get back until three o'clock in the morn. JEEEZ! What happened to him!?!
We met Carl Sagan! It was GREAT!
Carl Sagan did THAT!
Naw! You don't understand. I'm gonna be on TV!
mumble mumble
...and he wants to read my river journals... start a correspondence!
Sure man, right!
I mean, this guy's brilliant!
Maybe we ought to go to "Mars" again, eh?
He's a
It's
Cosmos
Unbelievable!
Forget "Mars", guys.. Y'all are weird enough already!
mumble mumble mumble mumble mumble mumble.....

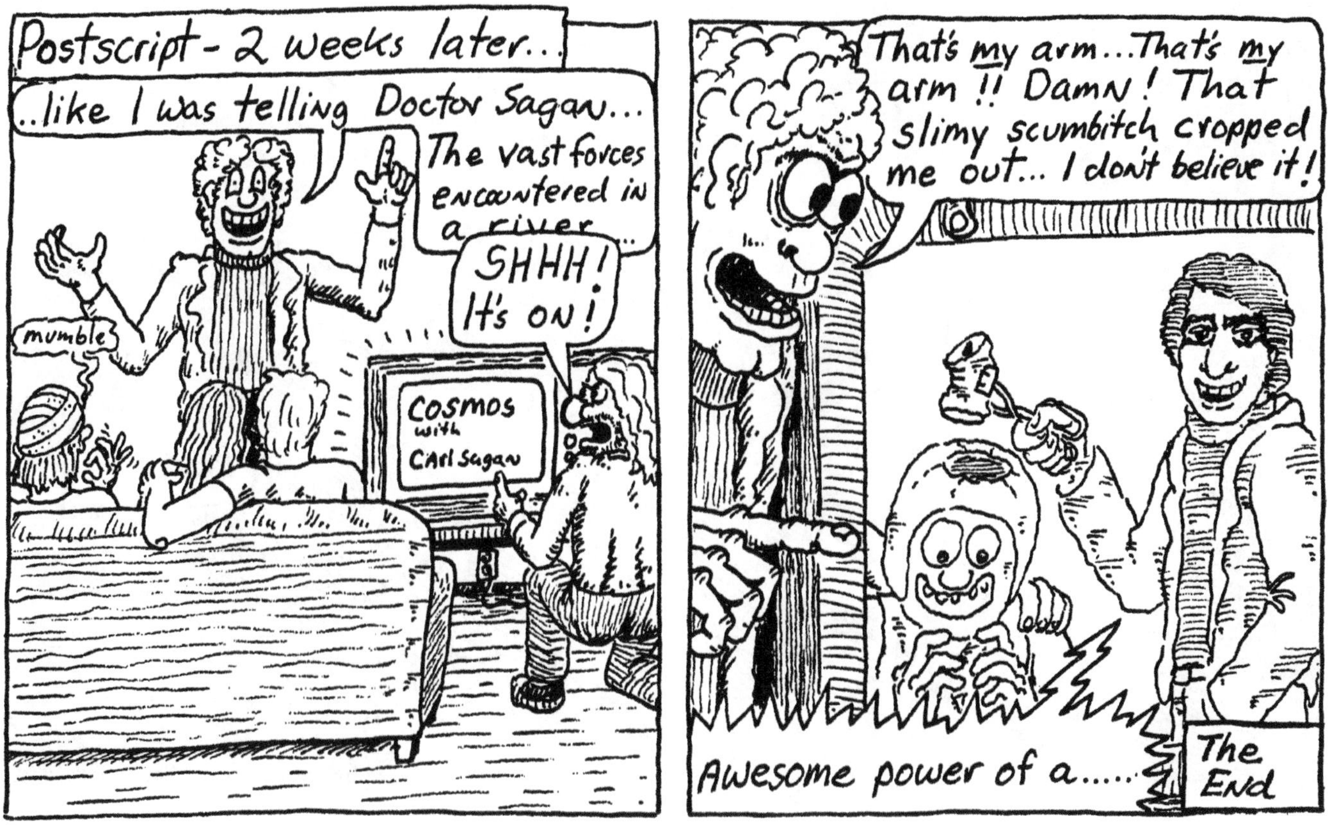

Postscript - 2 weeks later...
..like I was telling Doctor Sagan...
The vast forces encountered in a river....
mumble
SHHH! It's ON!
COSMOS with CArl Sagan
That's my arm... That's my arm!! Damn! That slimy scumbitch cropped me out... I don't believe it!
Awesome power of a.....
The End

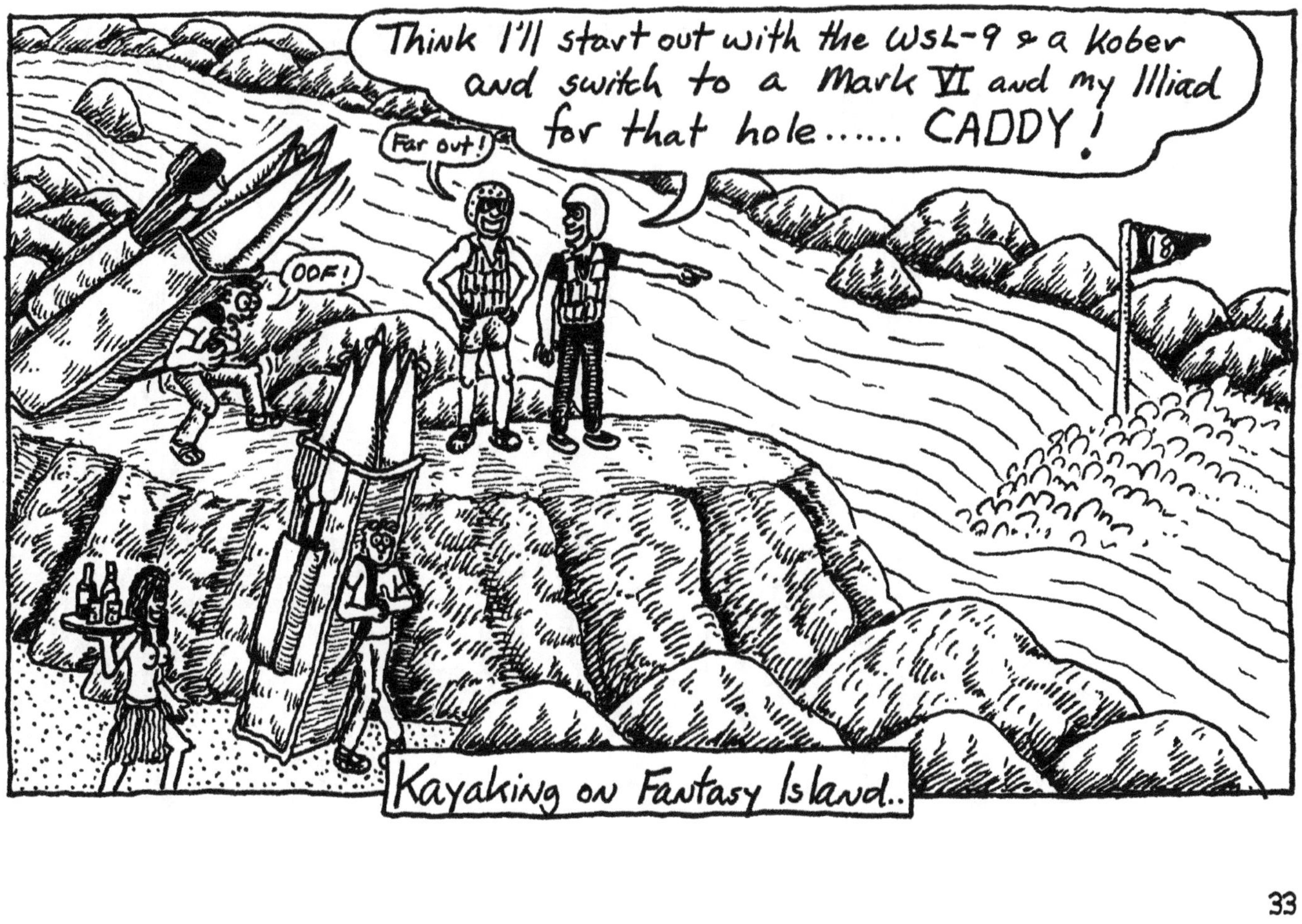

Think I'll start out with the WSL-9 & a Kober and switch to a Mark VI and my Illiad for that hole...... CADDY!
Far out!
OOF!
18
Kayaking on Fantasy Island..

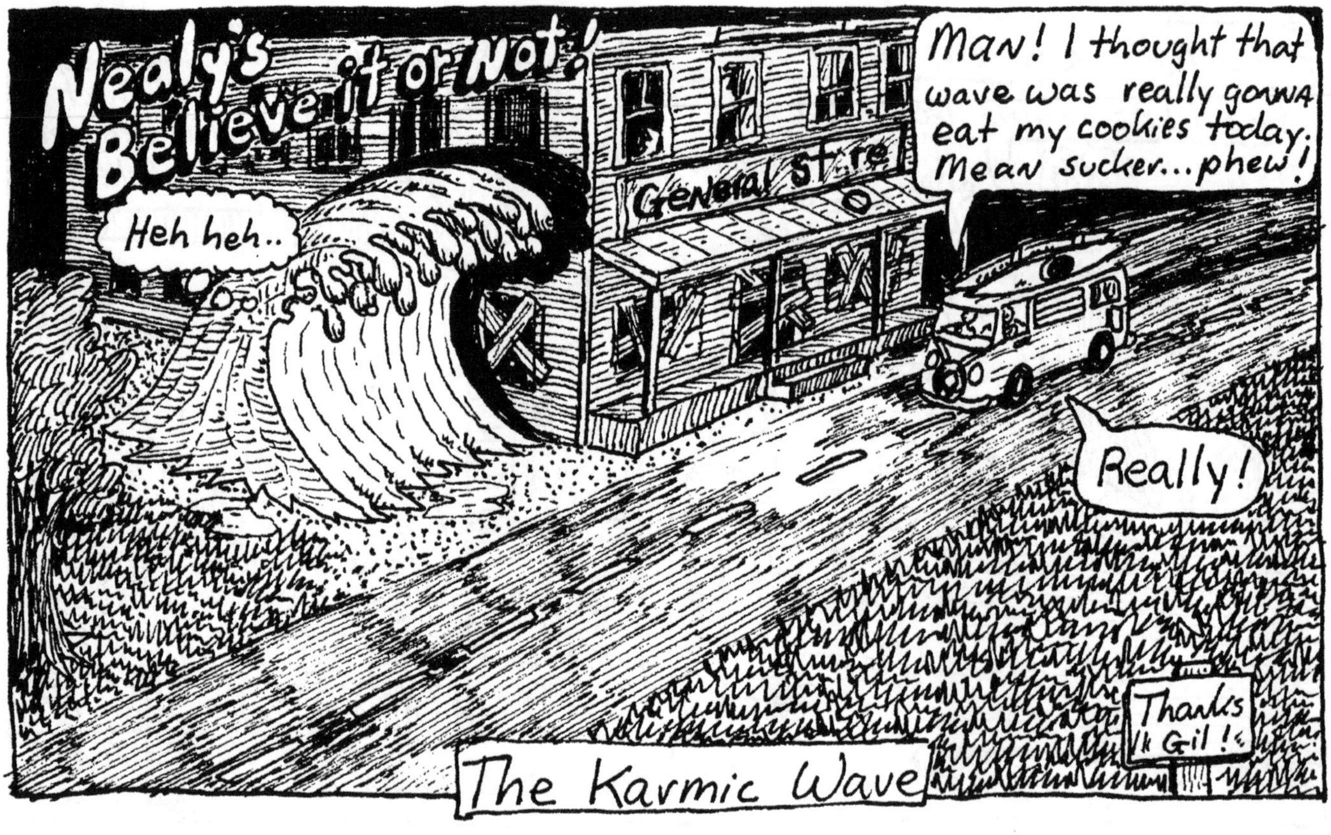
Nealy's Believe it or Not!
General Store
Heh heh..
Man! I thought that wave was really gonna eat my cookies today. Mean sucker...phew!
Really!
Thanks Gil!
The Karmic Wave

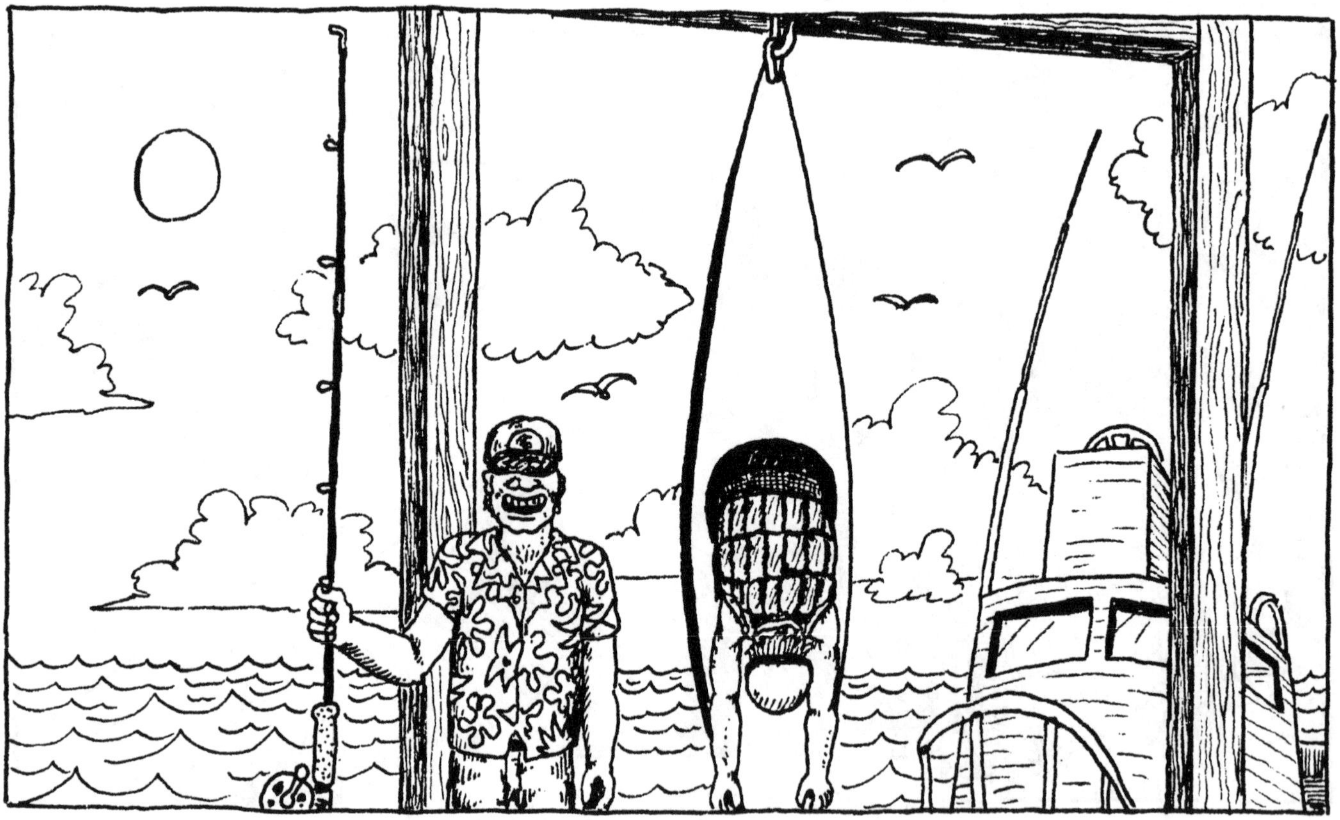

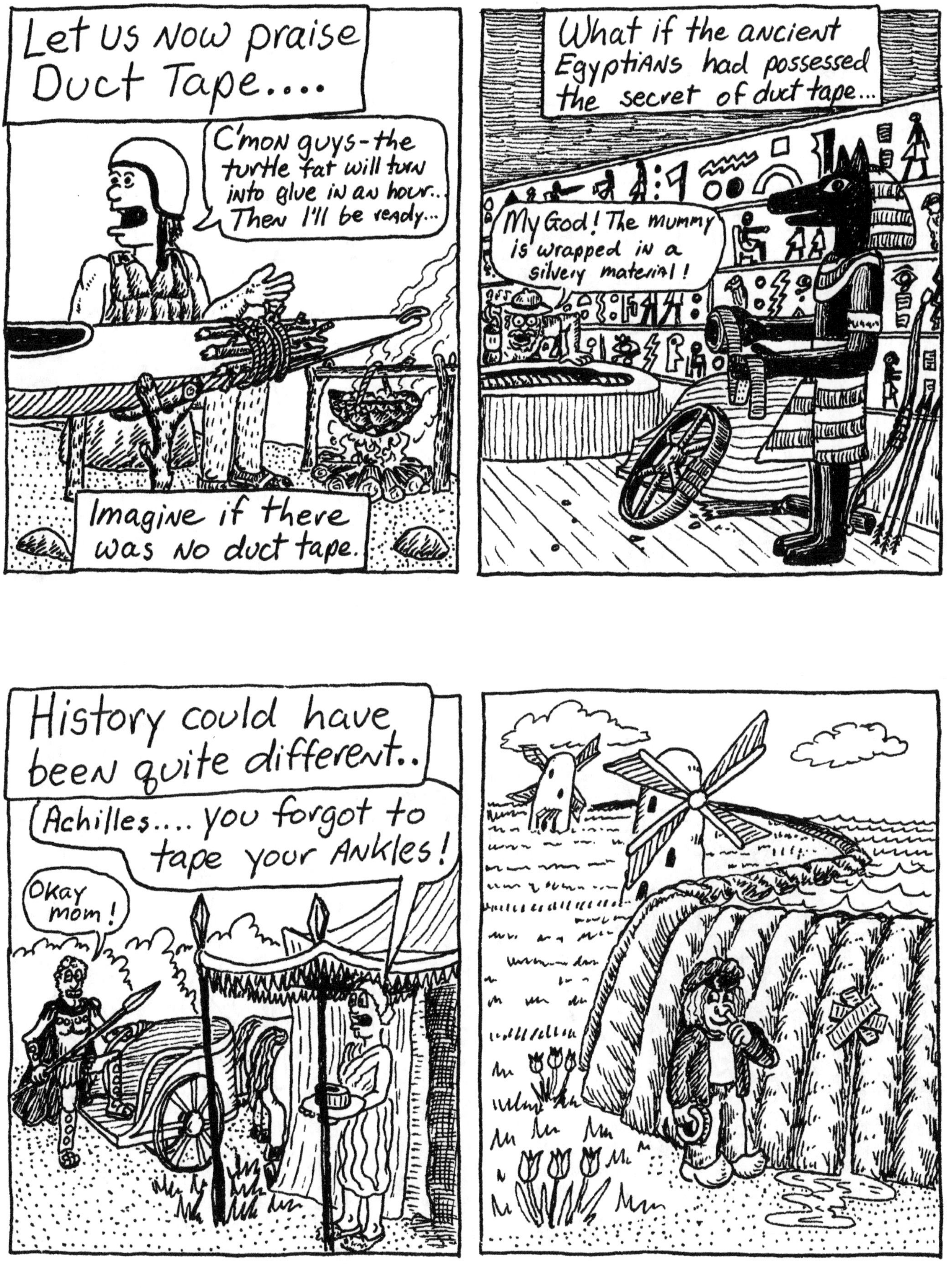
Let us now praise Duct Tape....
C'mon guys-the turtle fat will turn into glue in an hour.. Then I'll be ready...
Imagine if there was no duct tape.
What if the ancient Egyptians had possessed the secret of duct tape...
My God! The mummy is wrapped in a silvery material!
History could have been quite different..
Achilles.... you forgot to tape your Ankles!
Okay mom!

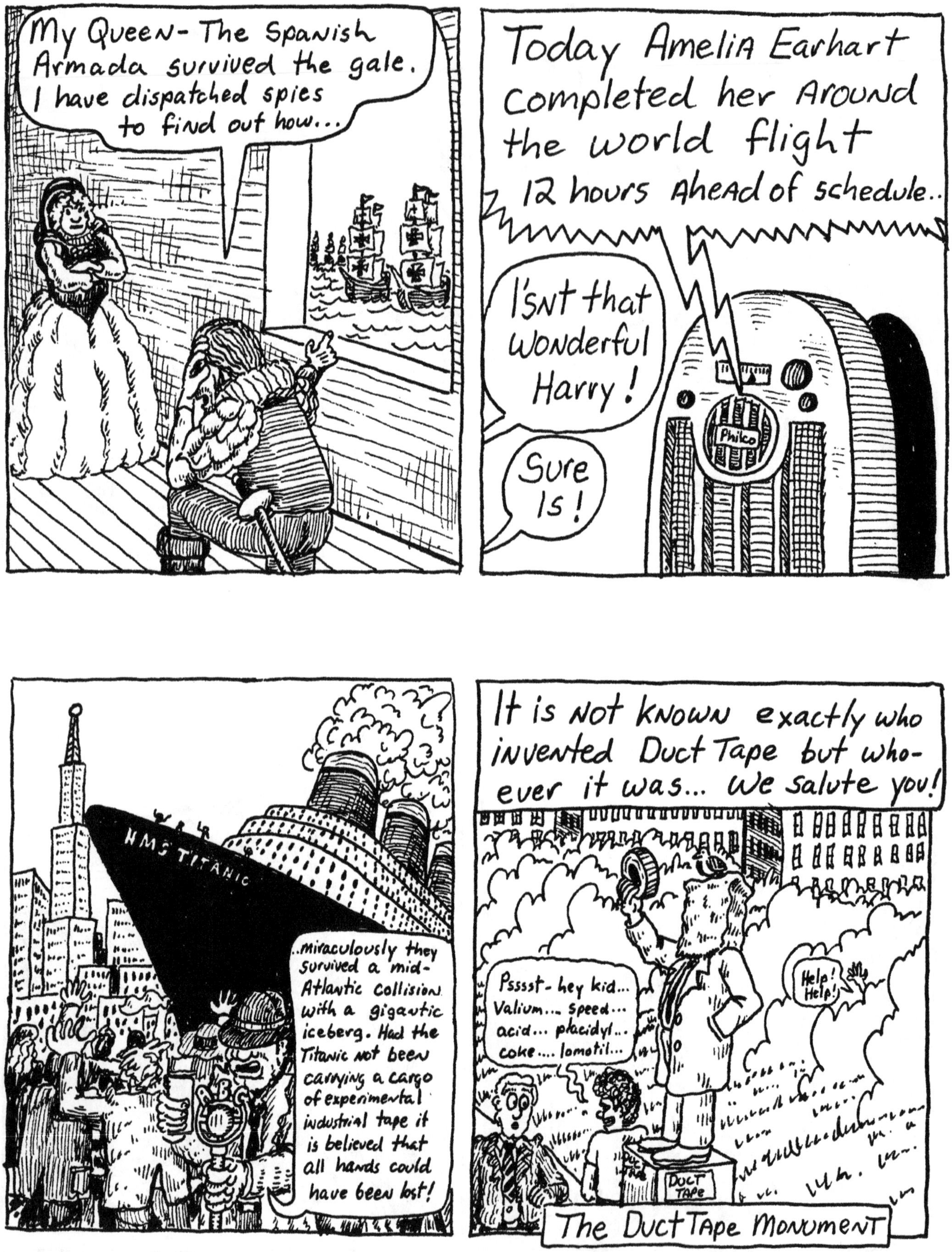
My Queen- The Spanish Armada survived the gale. I have dispatched spies to find out how...
Today Amelia Earhart completed her Around the world flight 12 hours Ahead of schedule..
I'snt that wonderful Harry!
Sure is!
Philco
HMS TITANIC
..miraculously they survived a mid-Atlantic collision with a gigantic iceberg. Had the Titanic not been carrying a cargo of experimental industrial tape it is believed that all hands could have been lost!
It is not known exactly who invented Duct Tape but who-ever it was... We salute you!
Psssst- hey kid... Valium... speed... acid... placidyl... coke.... lomotil...
Help! Help!
DUCT TAPE
The Duct Tape Monument

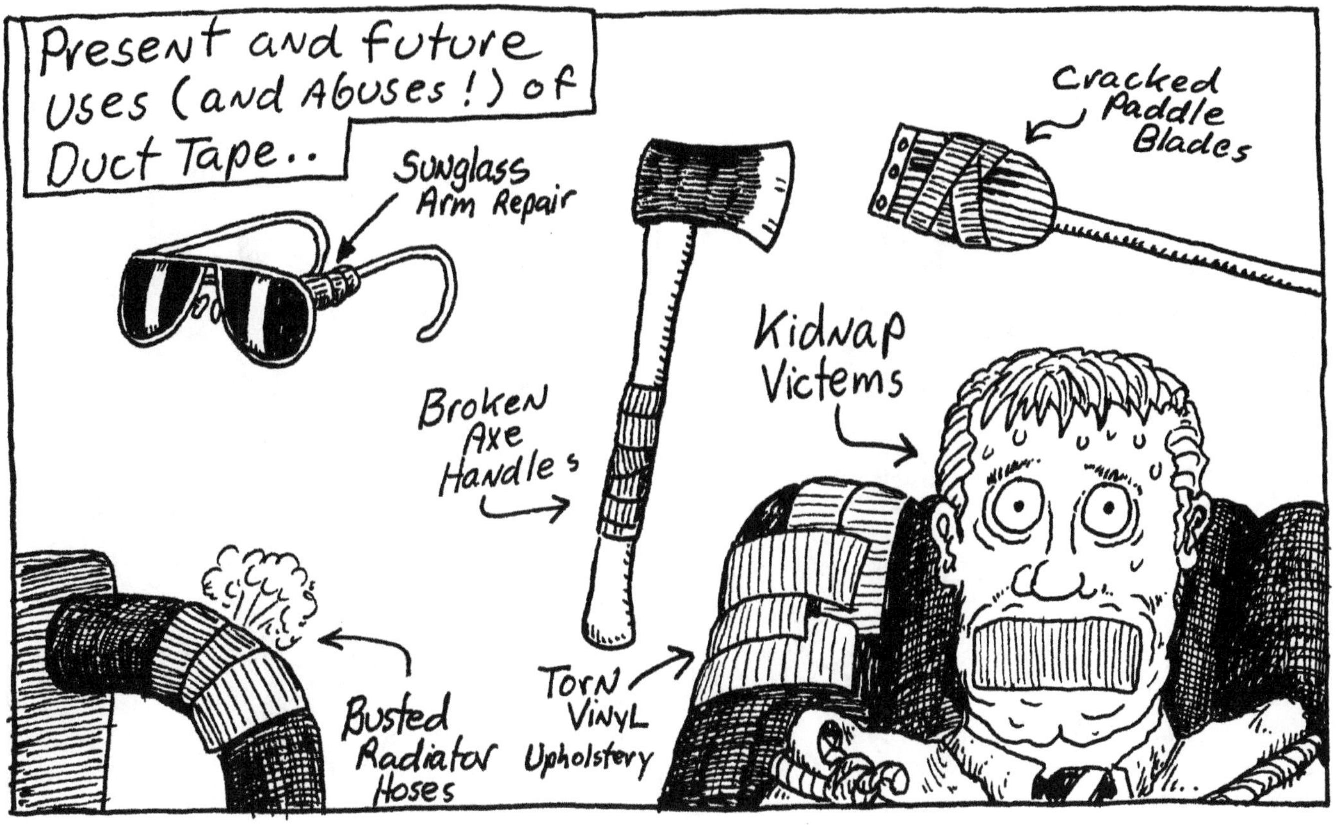
Present and future uses (and Abuses!) of Duct Tape..
Sunglass Arm Repair
Broken Axe Handles
Cracked Paddle Blades
Kidnap Victems
Busted Radiator Hoses
Torn Vinyl Upholstery

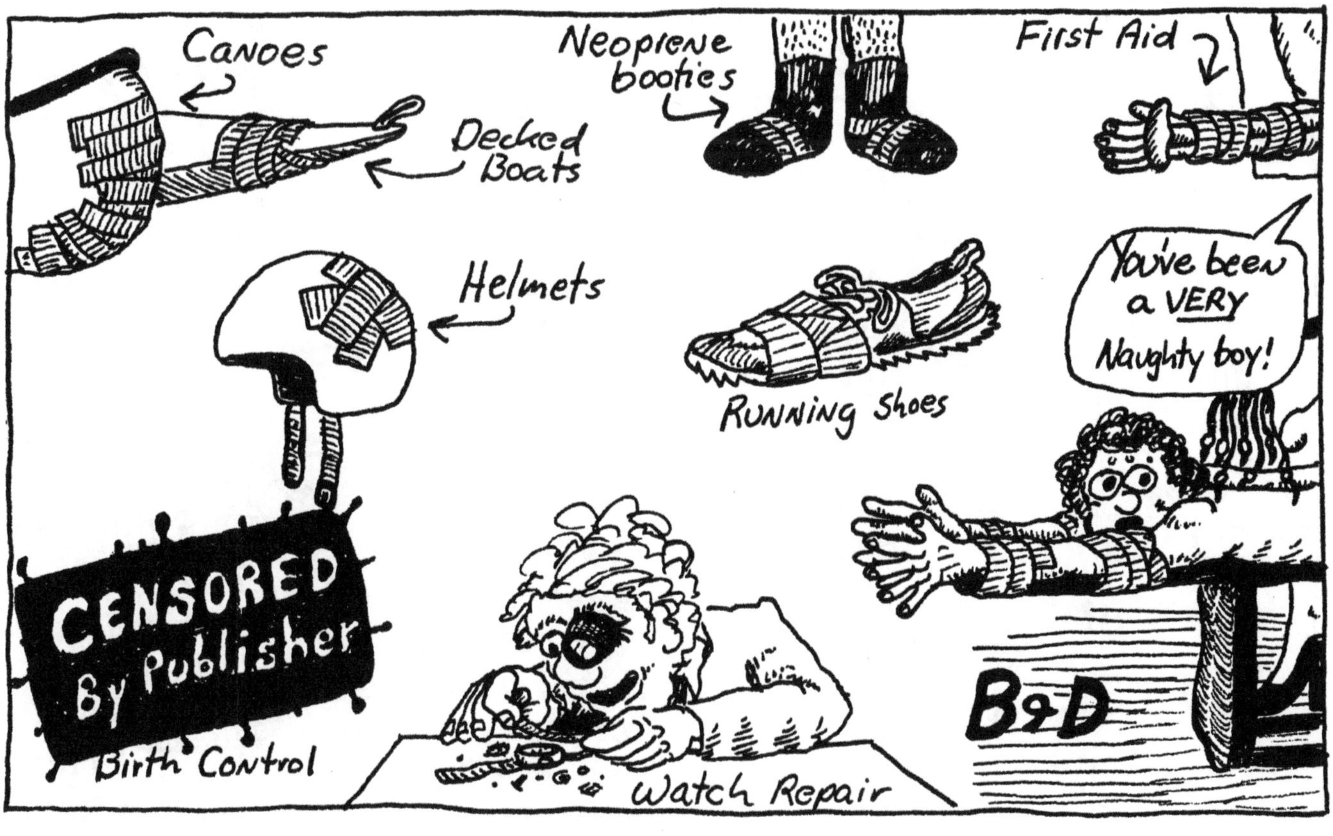
Canoes
Decked Boats
Neoprene booties
First Aid
Helmets
Running Shoes
You've been a VERY Naughty boy!
CENSORED By Publisher
Birth Control
Watch Repair
B&D

..One Giant Leap for Mankind..
RRRIIIPP!
Whoops...
Commander Armstrong.. This is mission Control- Quick! The Duct Tape!
Frequently its use has been hidden from the American Public!
Duct tape has been used for years by British rockclimbers to secure chocks in shallow cracks and rugosities..
Go for it, Mate!
Some things you can make with duct tape...
Water bottle converted to thermos by wrapping with ethafoam & covering with duct tape.
Great for parties-Make a mold out of balled-up Newspaper, tape it up, remove the paper and voila'.... Silver Cowboy Boots
Handy belt-loop for flashlight
Nylon cord
Duct tape
This T-shirt design is easily converted to a Western-style vest- Just cut along the dotted line- Perfect with the cowboy boots!
—CUT
THE END

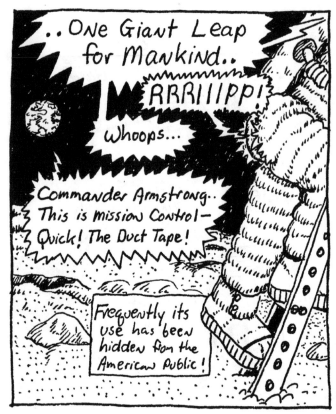

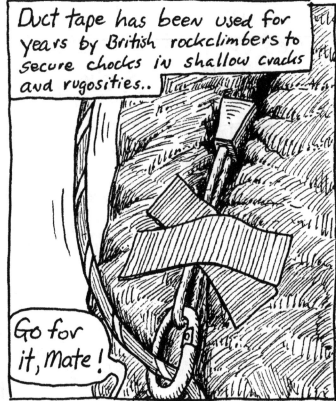

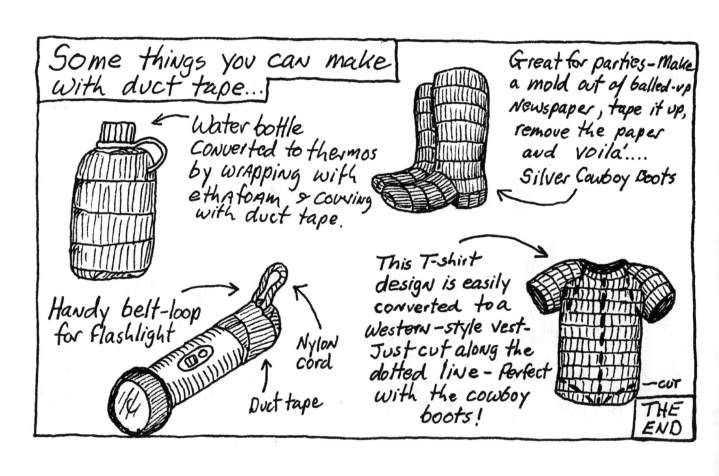

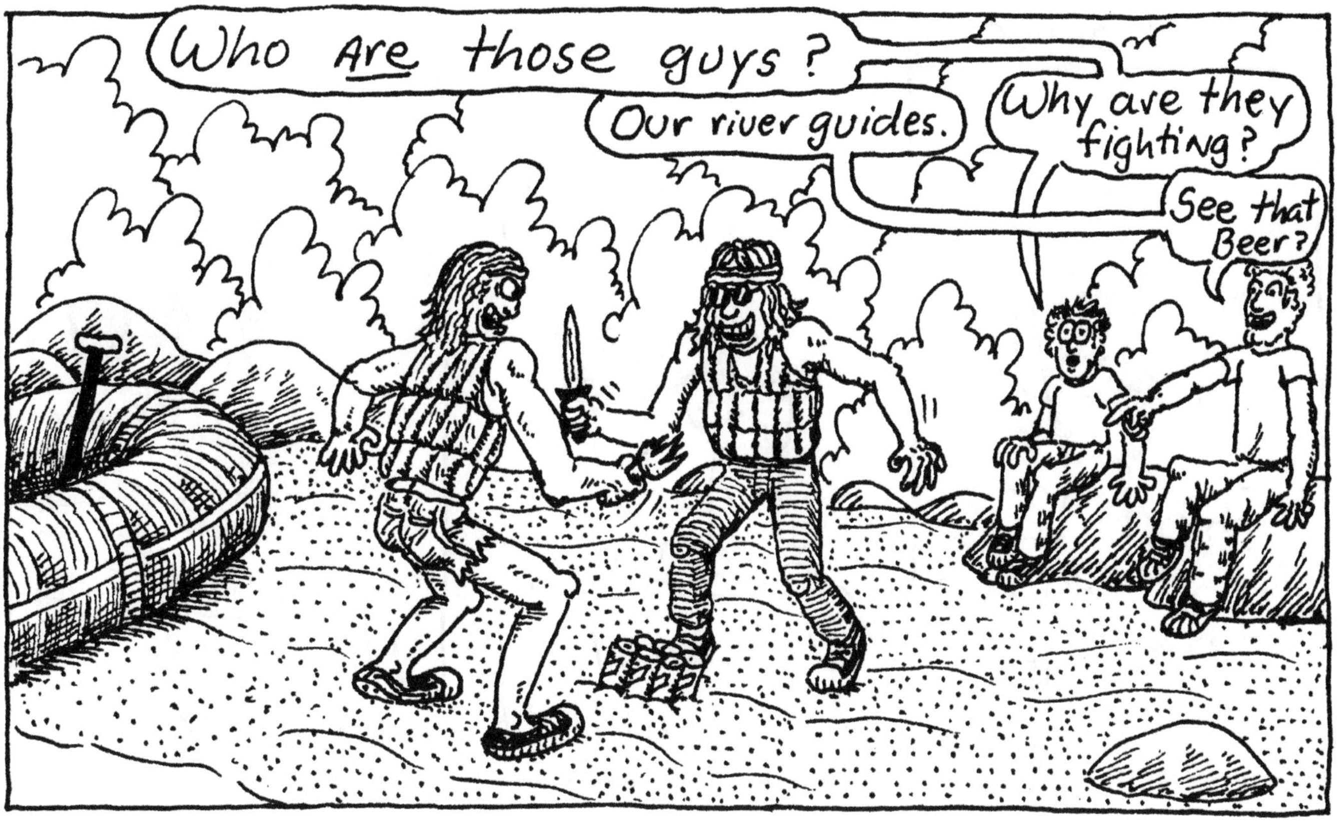
Who ARE those guys?
Our river guides.
Why are they fighting?
See that Beer?

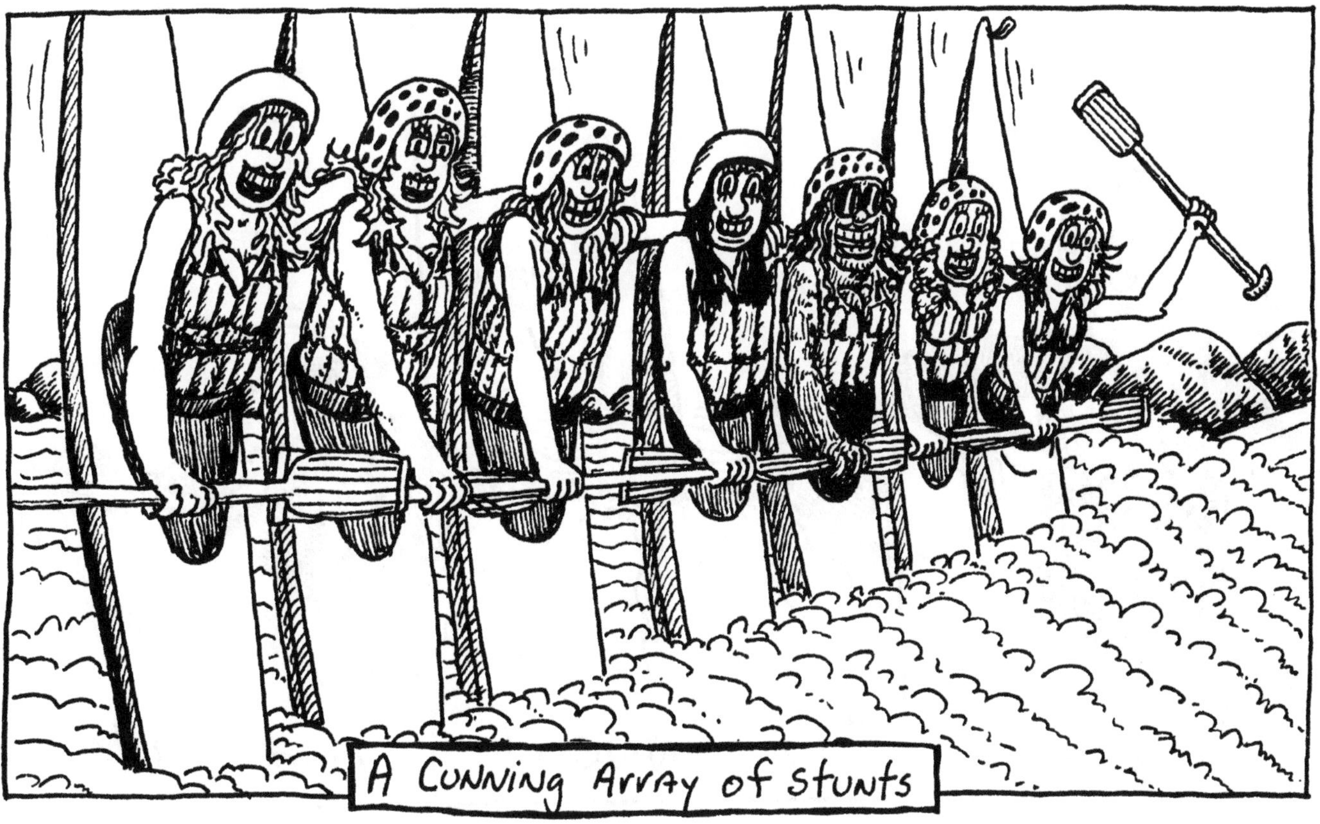
A CUNNING ArrAy of StUNTS

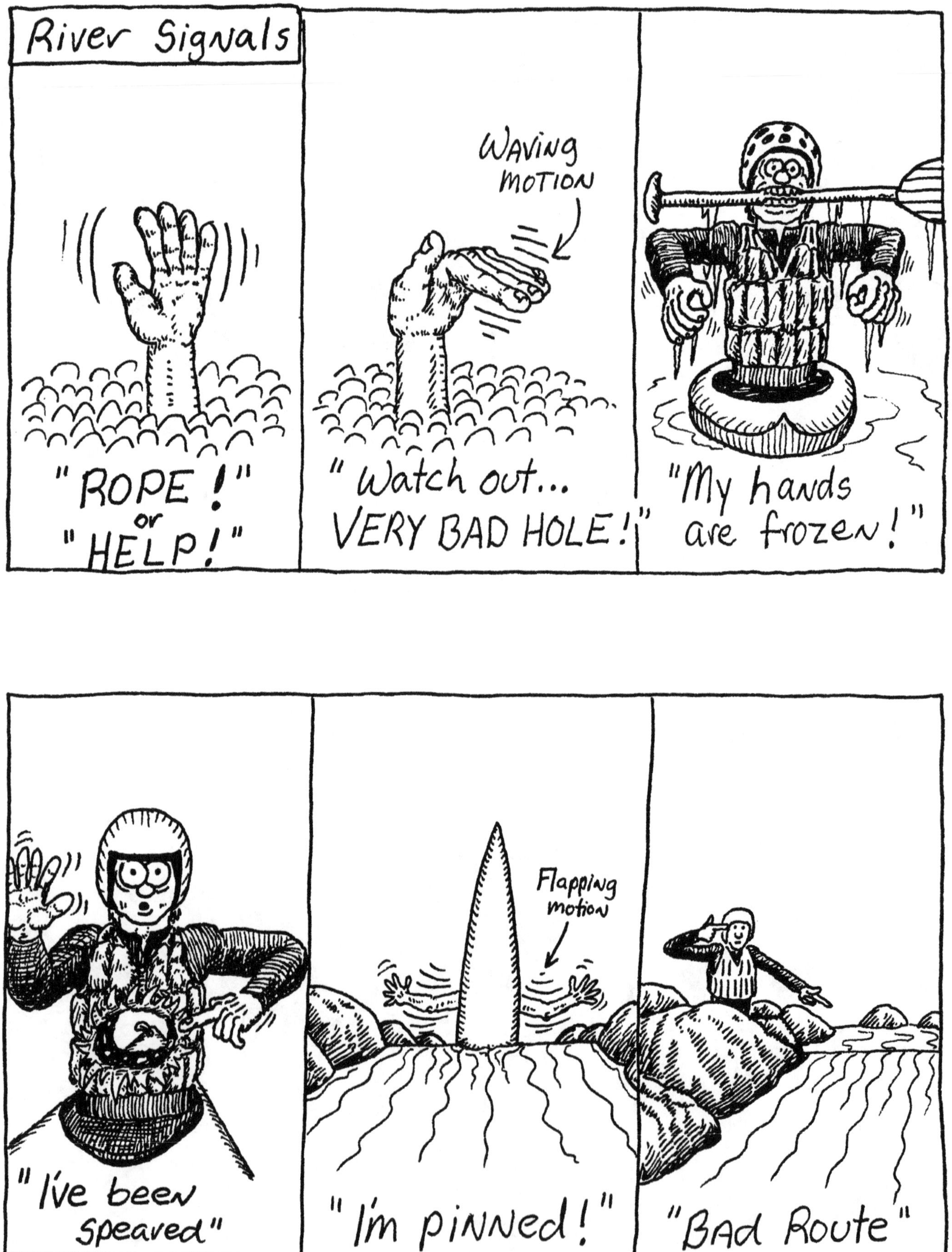
River Signals
"ROPE!" or "HELP!"
WAVING MOTION
"Watch out... VERY BAD HOLE!"
"My hands are frozen!"
"I've been speared"
Flapping motion
"I'm pinned!"
"BAd Route"

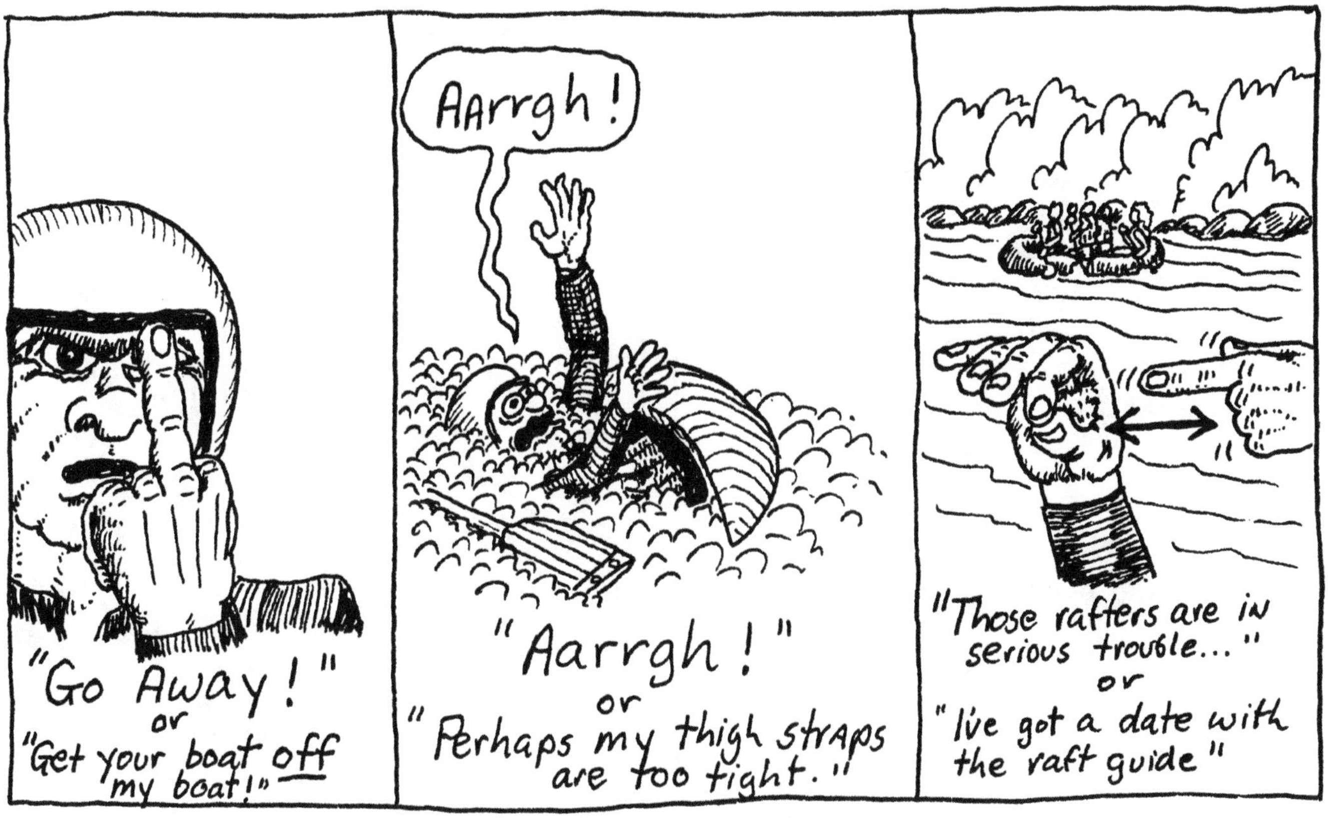
"Go Away!"
or
"Get your boat off my boat!"
Aarrgh!
"Aarrgh!"
or
"Perhaps my thigh straps are too tight."
"Those rafters are in serious trouble..."
or
"I've got a date with the raft guide"

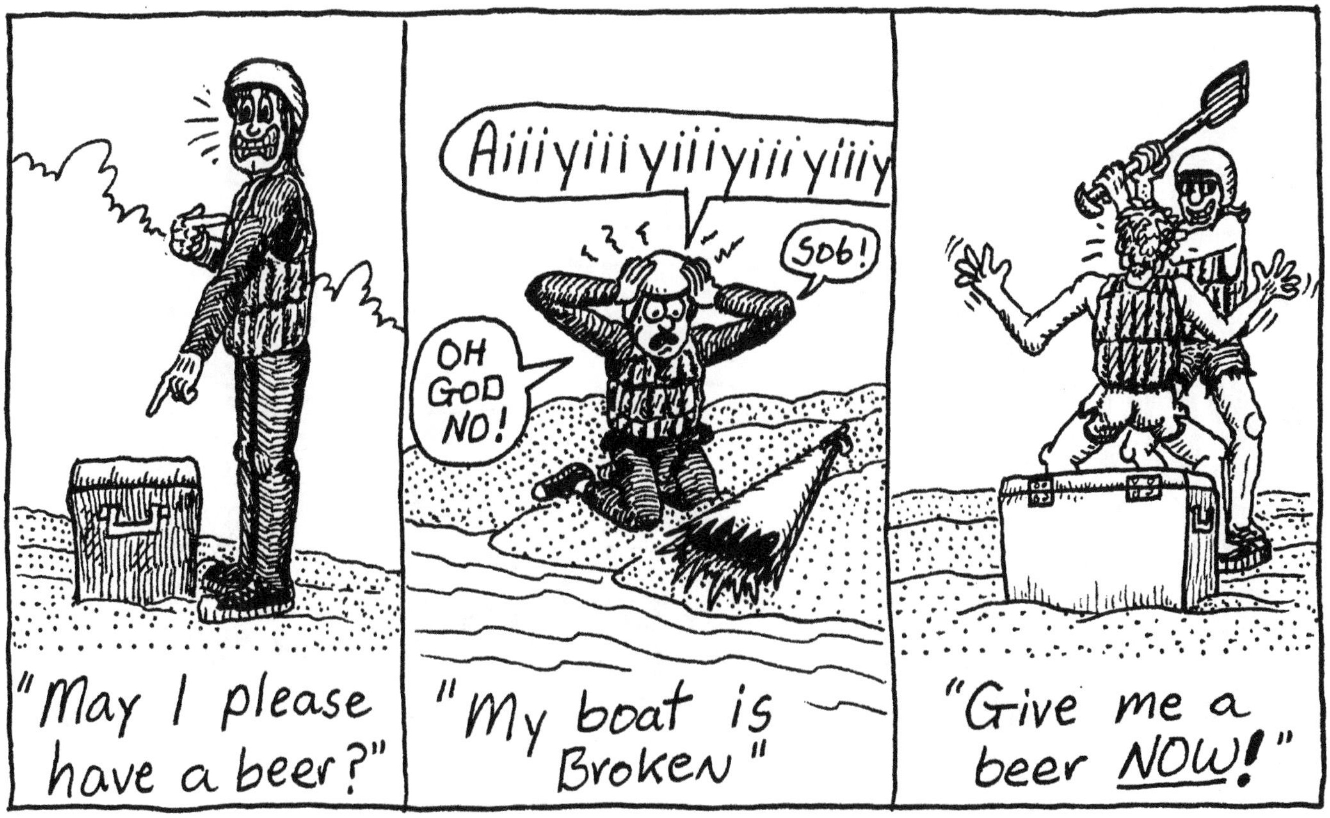
"May I please have a beer?"
Aiiiyiiiyiiiyiiiyiiiy
Sob!
OH GOD NO!
"My boat is Broken"
"Give me a beer NOW!"

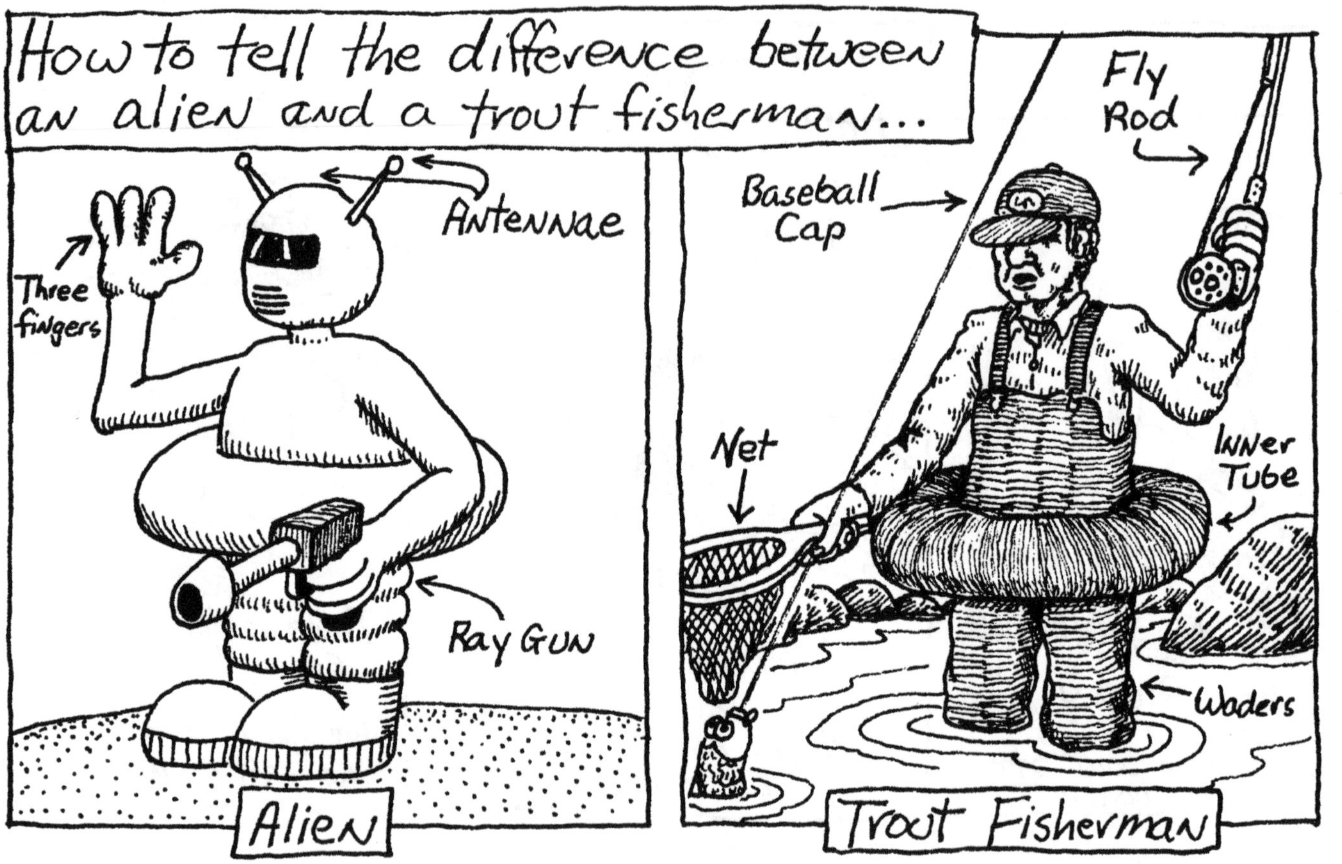
How to tell the difference between an alien and a trout fisherman...
Antennae
Three fingers
Ray Gun
Alien
Fly Rod
Baseball Cap
Net
Inner Tube
Waders
Trout Fisherman

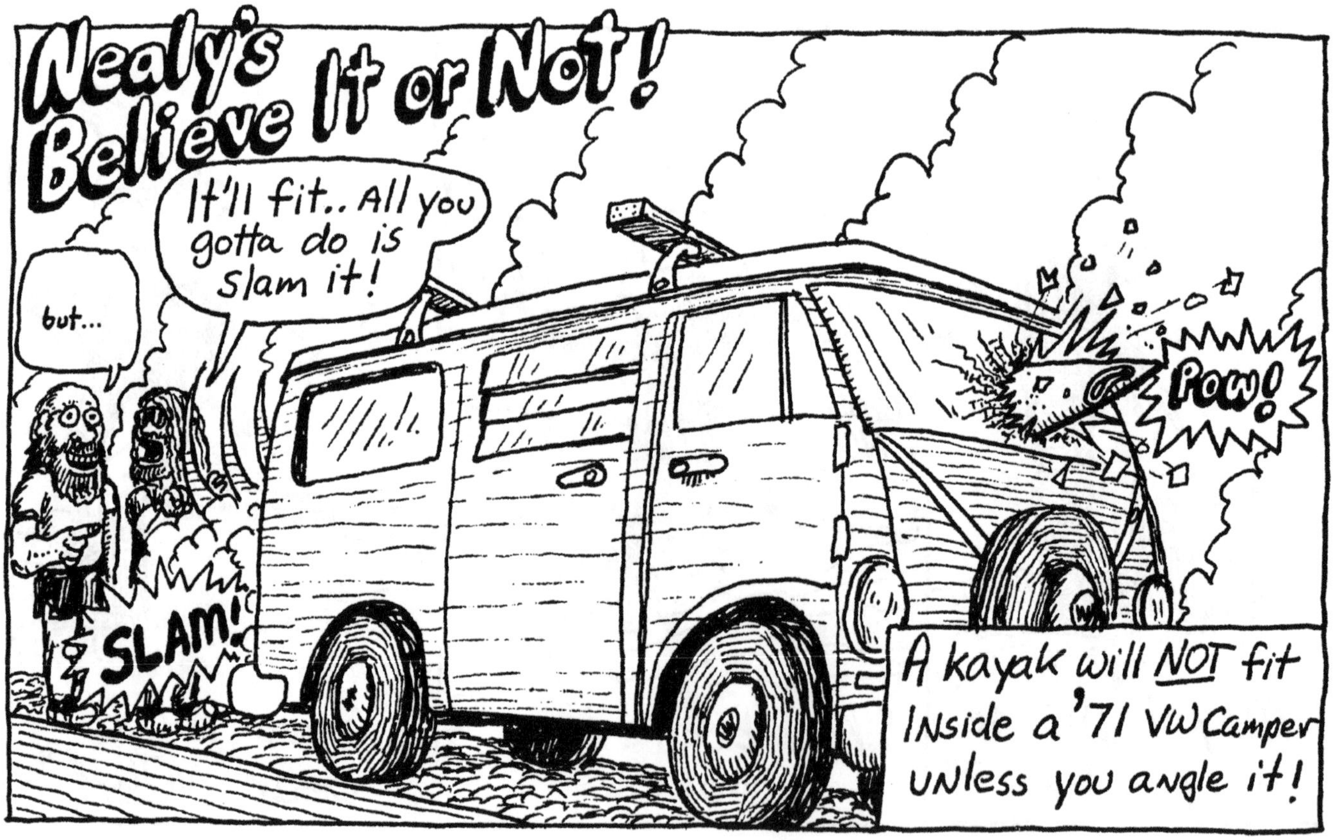
Nealy's Believe It or Not!
but...
It'll fit.. All you gotta do is slam it!
SLAM!
POW!
A kayak will NOT fit Inside a '71 VW Camper unless you angle it!

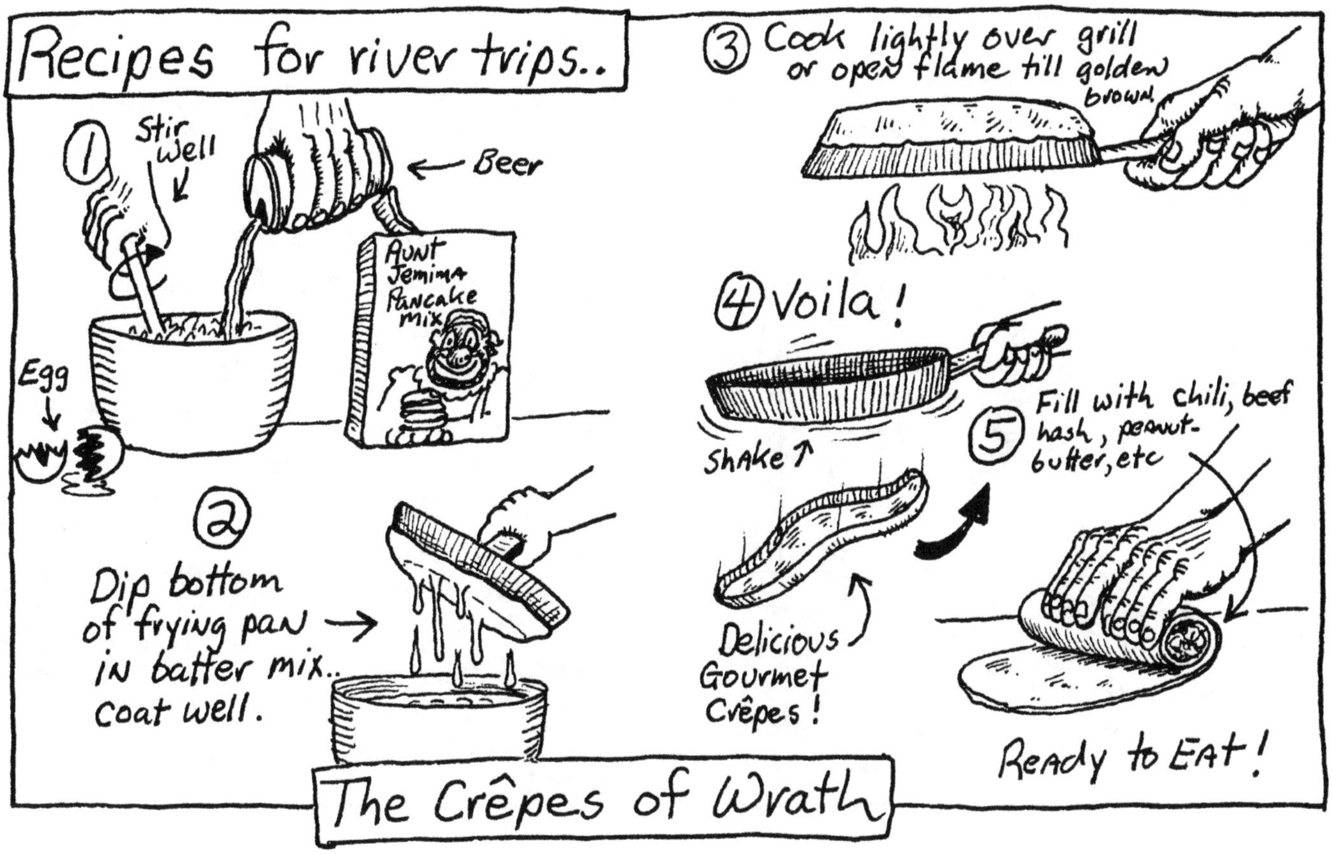
Recipes for river trips..
① Stir well
Beer
Egg
Aunt Jemima Pancake mix
② Dip bottom of frying pan in batter mix.. coat well.
③ Cook lightly over grill or open flame till golden brown
④ Voila!
Shake ↑
Delicious Gourmet Crêpes!
⑤ Fill with chili, beef hash, peanut-butter, etc
Ready to EAT!
The Crêpes of Wrath

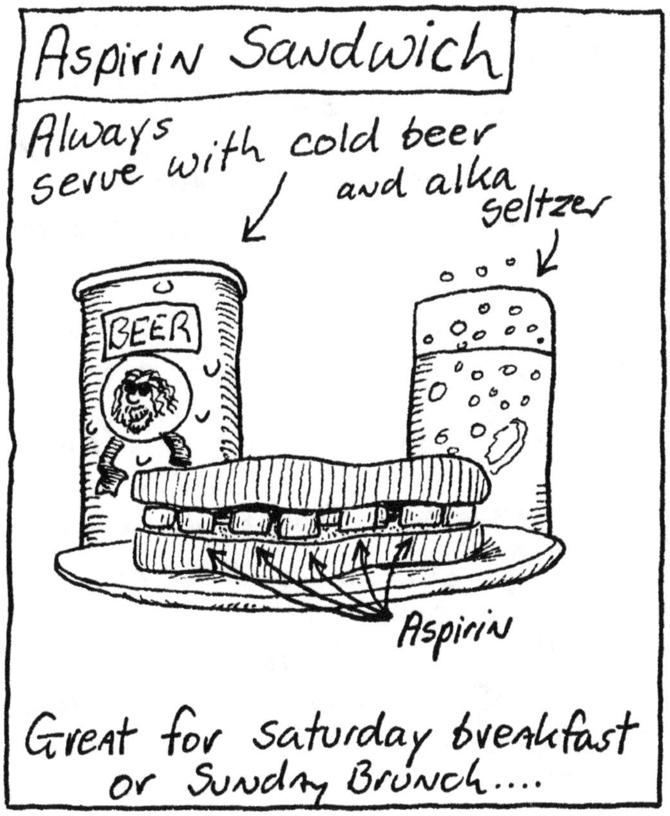
Aspirin Sandwich
Always serve with cold beer
and alka seltzer
BEER
Aspirin
Great for saturday breakfast or Sunday Brunch....

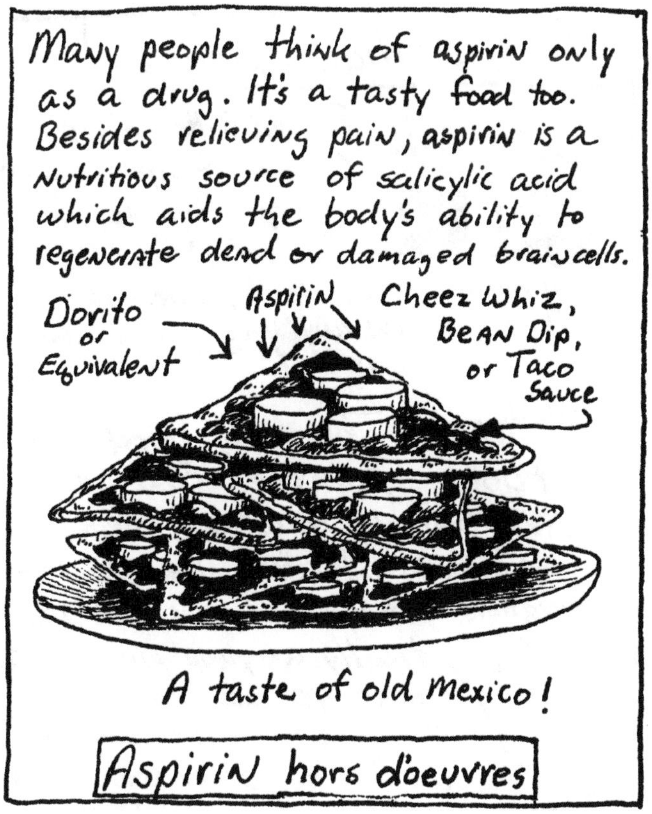
Many people think of aspirin only as a drug. It's a tasty food too. Besides relieving pain, aspirin is a Nutritious source of salicylic acid which aids the body's ability to regenerate dead or damaged braincells.
Dorito or Equivalent
Aspirin
Cheez Whiz, Bean Dip, or Taco Sauce
A taste of old Mexico!
Aspirin hors d'oeuvres

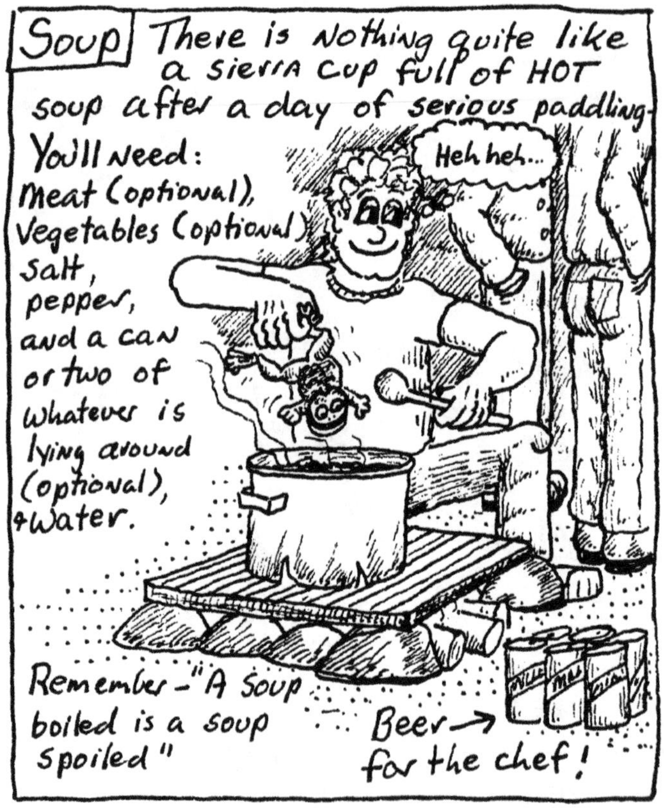
Soup
There is Nothing quite like a sierra cup full of HOT soup after a day of serious paddling.
You'll need:
Meat (optional),
Vegetables (optional)
salt,
pepper,
and a can or two of whatever is lying around (optional),
& water.
Heh heh...
Remember-"A soup boiled is a soup spoiled"
Beer → for the chef!

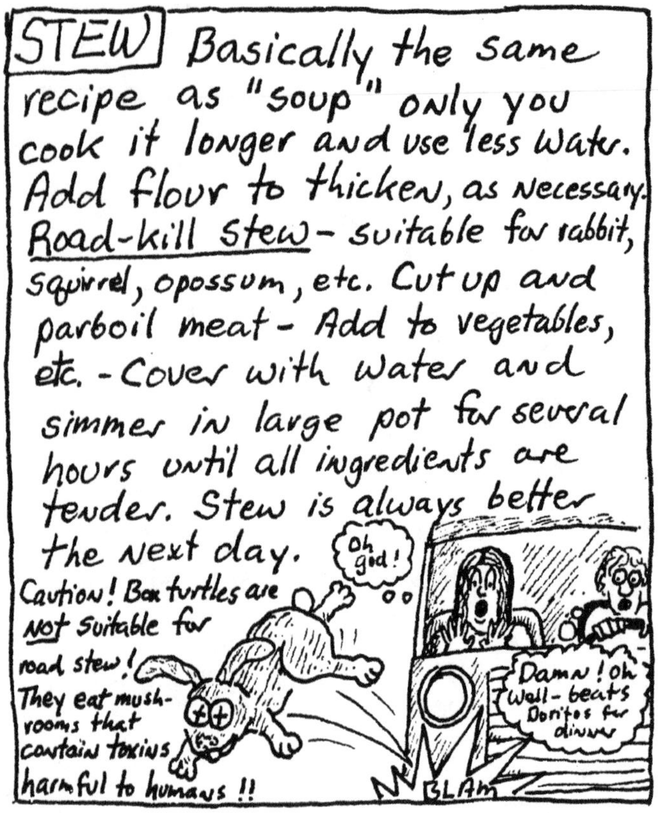
STEW
Basically the same recipe as "soup" only you cook it longer and use less water. Add flour to thicken, as necessary.
Road-kill stew - suitable for rabbit, squirrel, opossum, etc. Cut up and parboil meat - Add to vegetables, etc. - Cover with water and simmer in large pot for several hours until all ingredients are tender. Stew is always better the next day.
Oh god!
Caution! Box turtles are not suitable for road stew! They eat mushrooms that contain toxins harmful to humans!!
Damn! Oh well - beats Doritos for dinner
BLAM

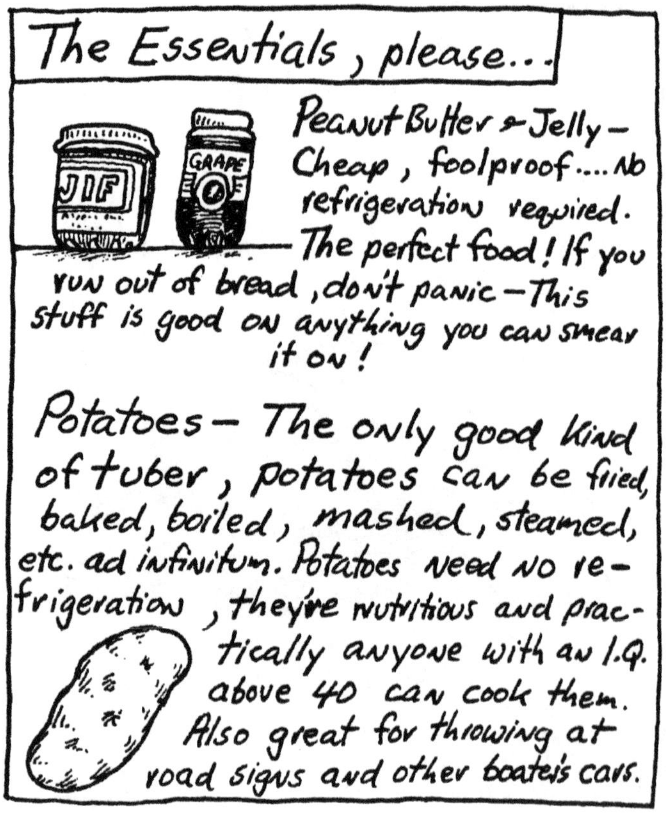
The Essentials, please...
JIF
GRAPE
Peanut Butter & Jelly - Cheap, foolproof.... No refrigeration required. The perfect food! If you run out of bread, don't panic - This stuff is good on anything you can smear it on!
Potatoes - The only good kind of tuber, potatoes can be fried, baked, boiled, mashed, steamed, etc. ad infinitum. Potatoes need no refrigeration, they're nutritious and practically anyone with an I.Q. above 40 can cook them. Also great for throwing at road signs and other boater's cars.

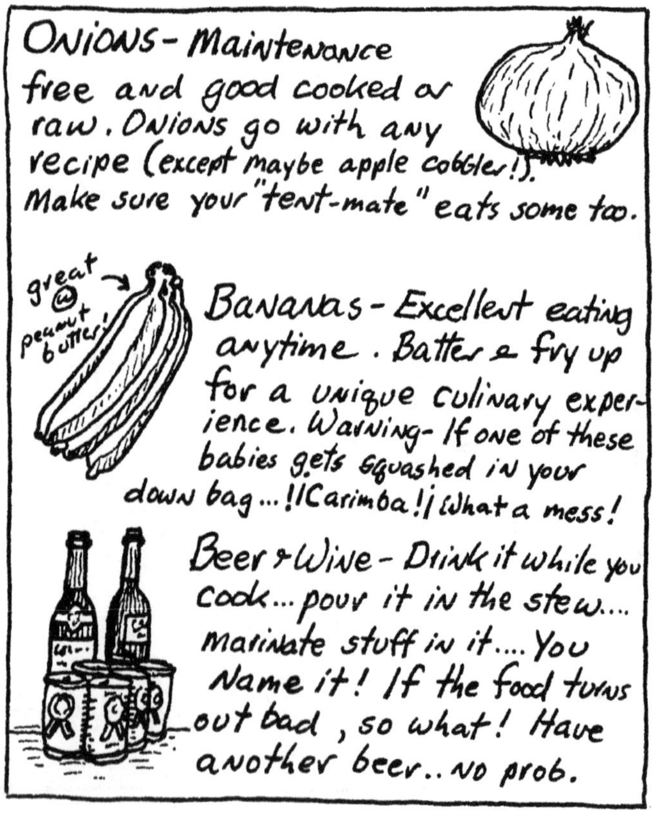
Onions - Maintenance free and good cooked or raw. Onions go with any recipe (except maybe apple cobbler!). Make sure your "tent-mate" eats some too.
great @ peanut butter! →
Bananas - Excellent eating anytime. Batter & fry up for a unique culinary experience. Warning - If one of these babies gets squashed in your down bag... ¡¡Carimba!¡ What a mess!
Beer & Wine - Drink it while you cook... pour it in the stew.... marinate stuff in it.... You name it! If the food turns out bad, so what! Have another beer.. no prob.

Helpful Hints-

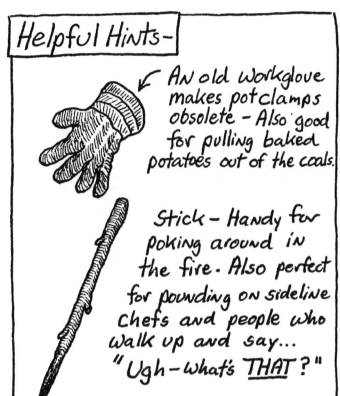

An old workglove makes pot clamps obsolete - Also good for pulling baked potatoes out of the coals.

Stick - Handy for poking around in the fire. Also perfect for pounding on sideline chefs and people who walk up and say...

"Ugh - what's *THAT*?"

Dogs are useful for wiping greasy hands on. They are also quite adept at pre-cleaning dirty pots & pans. These self-contained garbage disposals are cheap and easy to maintain. Koreans like them boiled or fried!

Gas - white or auto-dangerous to transport and use but what the hell. Gas (a.k.a. "hamburger helper") is the only way to ignite wet wood. Good Luck.

Ice Chest - don't scrimp, get a good big one that two people can sit on w/o breaking. Try to buy food that doesn't require refrigeration so the beer & wine isn't too crowded. Keep ice well-drained and it will last longer.

The Missing Link

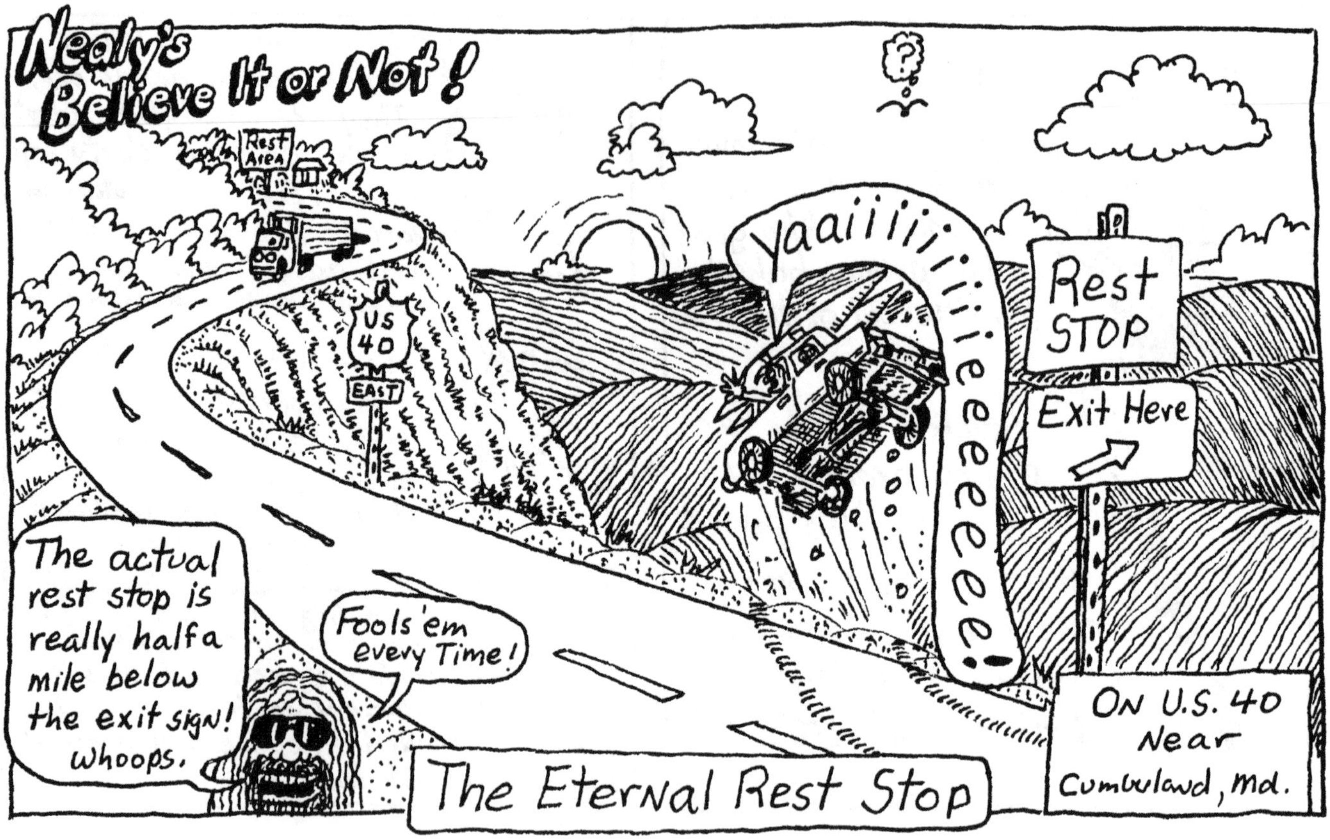
Nealy's Believe It or Not!
Rest Area
US 40 EAST
Yaaiiiiiiiiiiiieeeeeeeee!
Rest STOP
Exit Here
The actual rest stop is really half a mile below the exit sign! whoops.
Fools'em every Time!
The Eternal Rest Stop
ON U.S. 40 Near Cumberland, md.

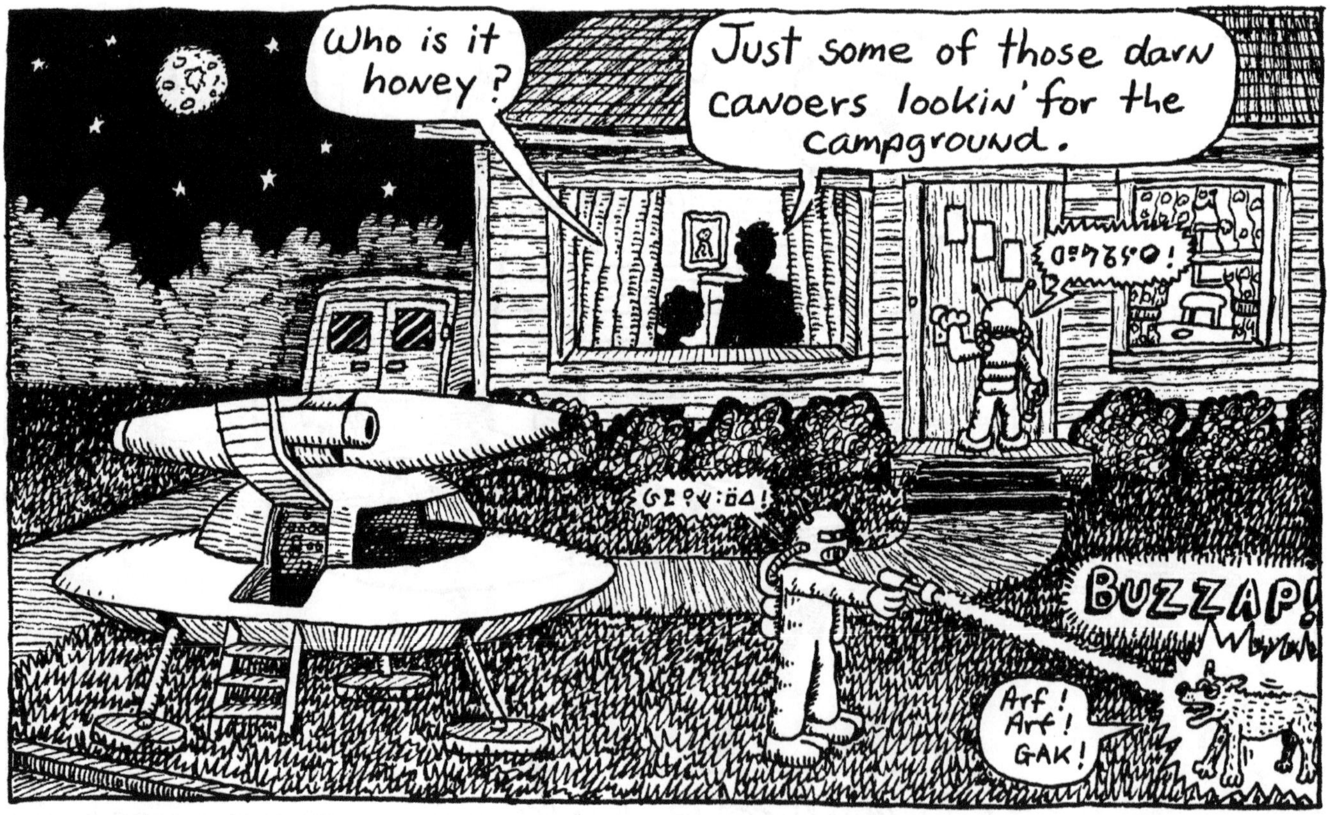
Who is it honey?
Just some of those darn canoers lookin' for the campground.
BUZZAP!
Arf! Arf! GAK!

Introduction to "C-boats; can't stay in 'em, can't live without 'em!" —

During my river travels over the past year, lots of disgruntled C-boaters have approached me and "suggested" that perhaps I should actually TRY a C-boat before casting stones at C-boaters in general. I rarely throw rocks at C-boaters and IF I do, it's at a particular one, not some general entity... REALLY!

OK guys, you win. I paddle one now (I'd be in it right now but "they" are making me write this!). My knees throb when the barometer drops... I can no longer walk unassisted at the take out. My ankles look like warthogs and I've got permanent cockpit creases on each hip. My elbows are hopelessly scarred. The condition of my hands is best left unsaid. My boat leaks like a WhiteHouse aide. I hate my bracing system. My paddle got terminally crunched yesterday... along with my shoulder. I talk endlessly about C-boats & "canoeing". I have joined the ranks of the living dead. I hope everyone is happy now. Never has a greater price been paid for objectivity!

[To my kayaking buddies: Don't worry — I haven't sold my kayak. I'm keeping it around for when the river floods and I totally wimp out. Sorry guys.]

The C-boat as a rescue tool—

Not The Paddle! Leggo, Damn It!

OK... look - if you let go I'll give you my BMW and my beach house... OK? Really - there's no sense in BOTH of us going over......

The C-boater can do little besides console the victim & offer psychological support...

Hey! You're gonna be JUST FINE! Don't worry - Get a good deep breath when you go off - I'll be down there real soon!

Oh yeah! Where'd you hide the keys to the shuttle car?

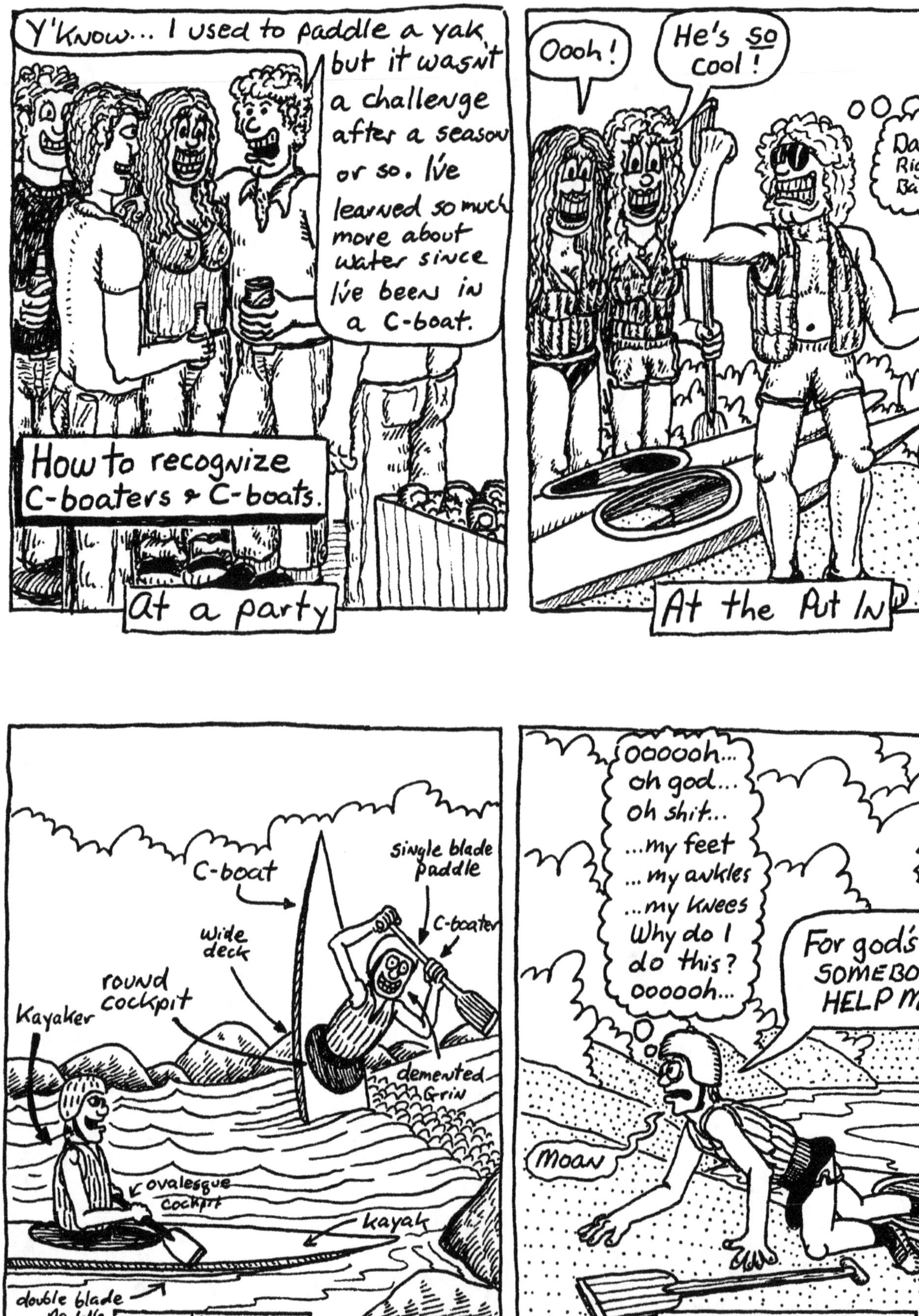
Y'Know... I used to paddle a yak, but it wasn't a challenge after a season or so. I've learned so much more about water since I've been in a C-boat.
How to recognize C-boaters & C-boats.
At a party
Oooh!
He's so cool!
Damn Right Baby
At the Put In
C-boat
single blade paddle
wide deck
C-boater
round cockpit
Kayaker
demented Grin
ovalesque cockpit
kayak
double blade paddle
On the river
oooooh... oh god... oh shit... ...my feet ...my ankles ...my knees Why do I do this? oooooh...
For god's sake SOMEBODY HELP ME!
Moan
At the take out

Hand Weights (min. 20 lb. each)

Whirlpool Attachment (optional)

gasp!

Cold Shower

Ice cubes

Sitting on feet!

C-boat practice at home

C-Boater's Pain Scale	
Zone 1 - Usually begins minutes after putting in. Mild foot cramps and a dull throbbing in the ankles and toes.	Zone 6 - Hideous Pain - If you get out of your boat you either (A) crawl around & moan, or (B) walk like the hunchback of Notre Dame. Note - few open boaters break this threshold.
Zone 2 - Characterized by a mild respite from the initial wave of Z-1 pain followed by a rapid onset of Z-1 symptoms that get progressively worse very quickly!	Zone 7 - Unbearable pain in the ankles that takes your mind off your knees. Similar to having icepicks jabbed into the top of the foot.
Zone 3 - Recognized by the beginning of knee pain coupled with intense shooting pain in the ankles. Note: Kayakers never go beyond Zone 3	Zone 8 - Unbearable pain in your knees that takes your mind off your ankles. Few other than C-boaters & Italian government officials ever experience this type of pain.
Zone 4 - Pain preceded by a numbness & tingling similar to having your foot go to sleep. A good time to get out of the boat and do jumping jacks on the nearest rock.	Zone 9 - Indescribable pain that tends to be generalized rather than the specific stab-like pain of zones 7 & 8. Concentrate on the takeout and cold beer.
Zone 5 - Terrible pain: The main way to ascertain if you're in Zone 5 is if the pain does not go away after being out of the boat for 3 minutes or more.	Zone 10 - Zone 9^3! - Overwhelming pain from the mid-thigh down coupled with high anxiety and an intense desire to leap out of the boat & die quietly.

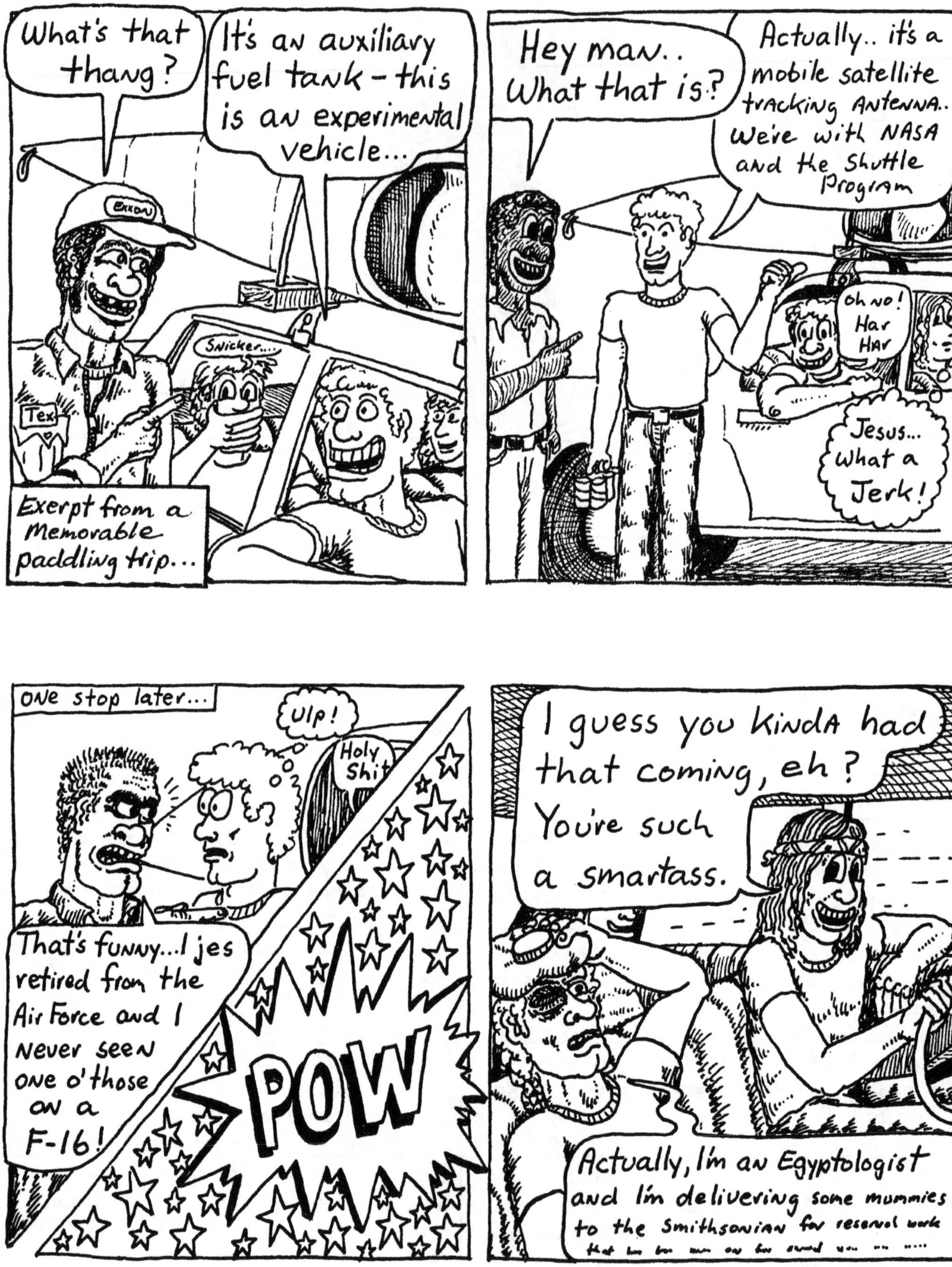

What's that thang?
It's an auxiliary fuel tank - this is an experimental vehicle...
Snicker...
Exerpt from a Memorable paddling trip...
Hey man.. What that is?
Actually.. it's a mobile satellite tracking ANTENNA... We're with NASA and the Shuttle Program
Oh no! Har Har
Jesus... What a Jerk!
ONE stop later...
Ulp!
Holy Shi
That's funny...I jes retired from the Air Force and I never seen one o'those on a F-16!
POW
I guess you kinda had that coming, eh? You're such a smartass.
Actually, I'm an Egyptologist and I'm delivering some mummies to the Smithsonian for research work

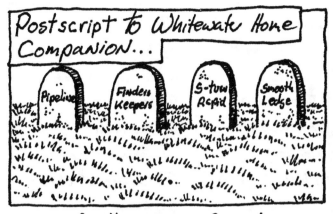

Postscript to Whitewater Home Companion...
Pipeline
Finders Keepers
S-turn Rapid
Smooth Ledge

Another Corps Coup!

It saddens me to report the untimely demise of several intimate acquaintances of mine - I refer to the numerous rapids inundated by a lake on the lower Haw River [See <u>Whitewater Home Companion</u> - pp 90, 93-94].

In order to obey the precepts of the Southern Recreational Lake Theorem ["Thou shalt not have to travel further than 50 miles in <u>any</u> direction without encountering a large lake"] the Army Corps has destroyed over half of one of the top whitewater runs in the state of North Carolina. To add insult to injury, it's <u>MY</u> home river.

In response to the lake we formed a river protection organization to try to force the state political machine to enforce existing state environmental protection regulations protecting the river. While trying to end the legal(!) dumping of thousands of gallons a day(!!) of raw sewage, formaldehyde, textile dyes, heavy metals, petroleum by-products, insecticides, etc. <u>into</u> the river we discovered that the state environmental agency didn't ask what was being dumped, just how much! There isn't even a space on the licensing form to state what is actually being dumped!!! I sincerely hope that Idi Amin and the A.E.C. don't get wind of this pearl of bureaucratic obscurantism or we'll have radioactive corpses floating down the river too...

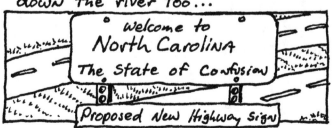

Welcome to
North Carolina
The State of Confusion
Proposed New Highway Sign

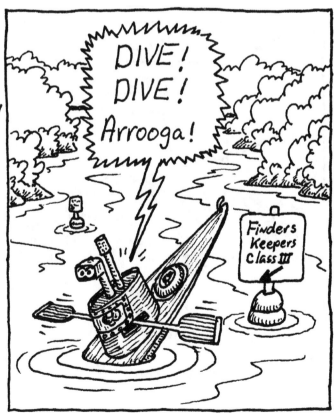

DIVE! DIVE! Arrooga!
Finders Keepers Class III

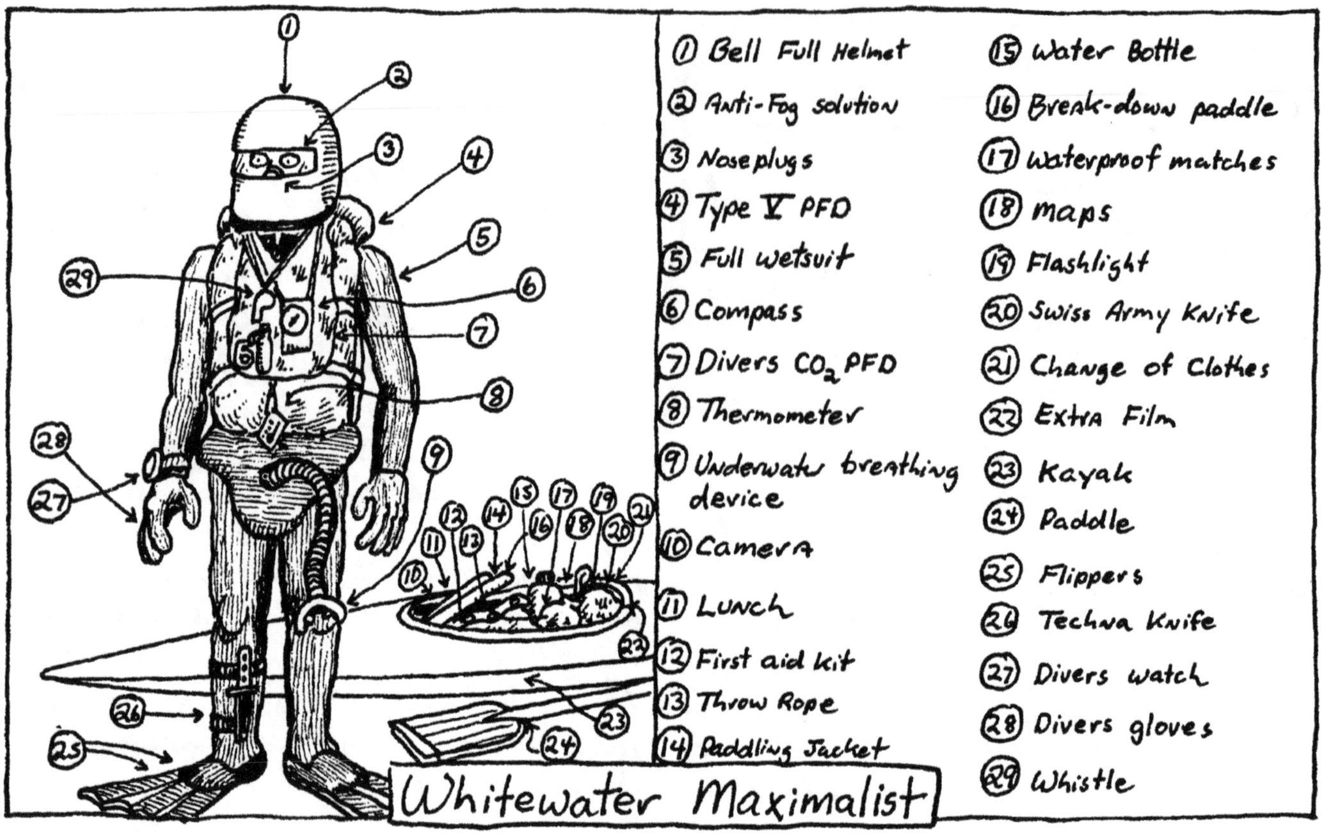

① Bell Full Helmet
② Anti-Fog solution
③ Noseplugs
④ Type V PFD
⑤ Full wetsuit
⑥ Compass
⑦ Divers CO_2 PFD
⑧ Thermometer
⑨ Underwater breathing device
⑩ Camera
⑪ Lunch
⑫ First aid kit
⑬ Throw Rope
⑭ Paddling Jacket
⑮ Water Bottle
⑯ Break-down paddle
⑰ waterproof matches
⑱ maps
⑲ Flashlight
⑳ Swiss Army Knife
㉑ Change of Clothes
㉒ Extra Film
㉓ Kayak
㉔ Paddle
㉕ Flippers
㉖ Techna Knife
㉗ Divers watch
㉘ Divers gloves
㉙ Whistle
Whitewater Maximalist

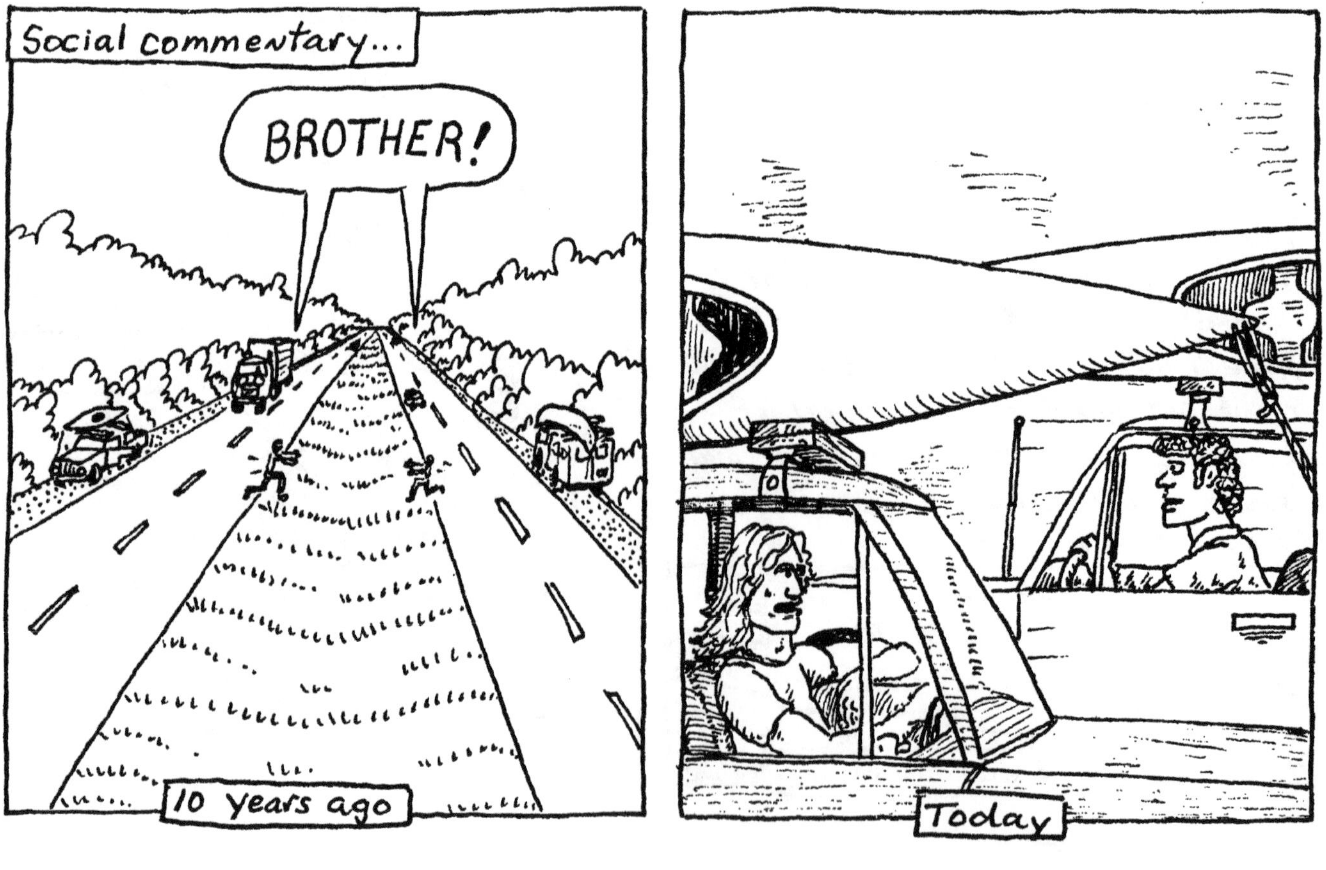

Social commentary...
BROTHER!
10 years ago
Today

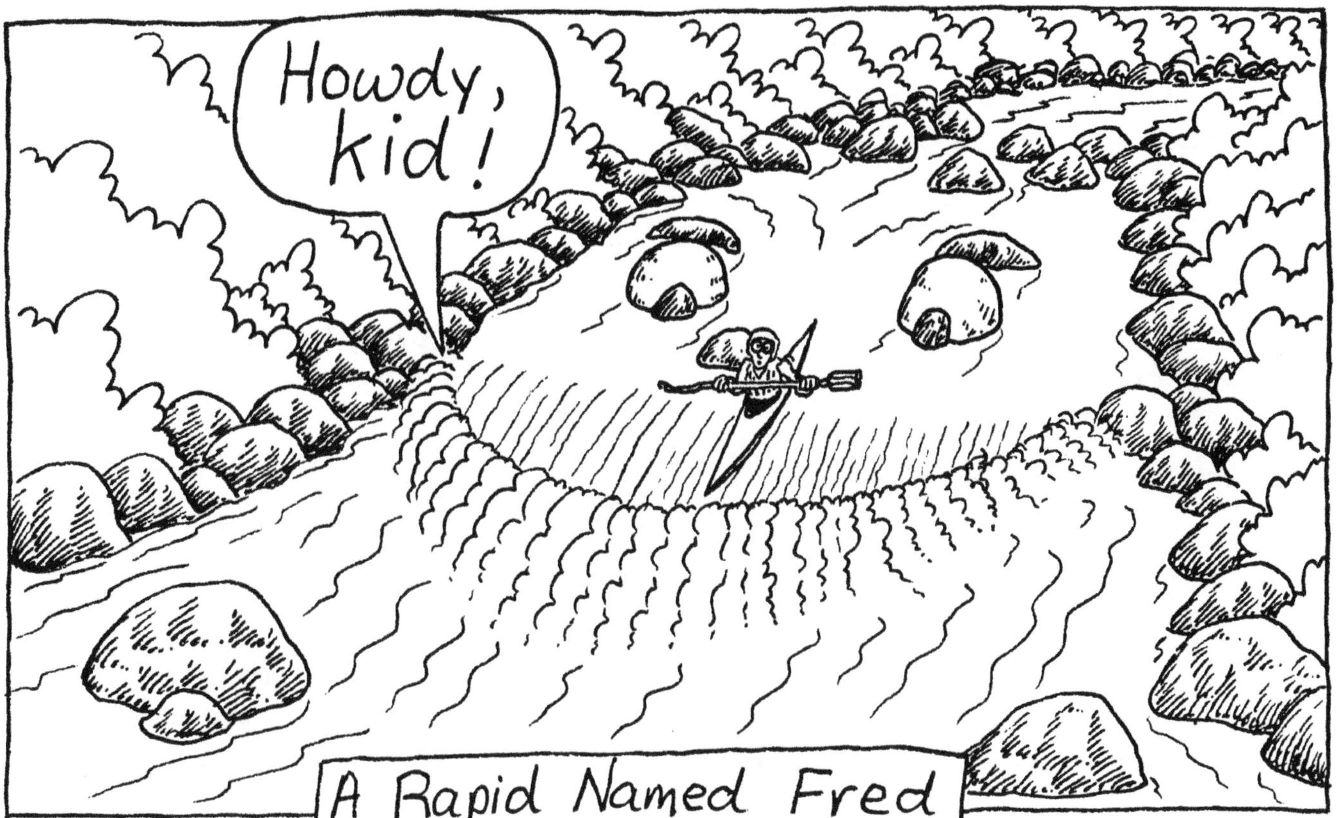
Howdy, kid!
A Rapid Named Fred

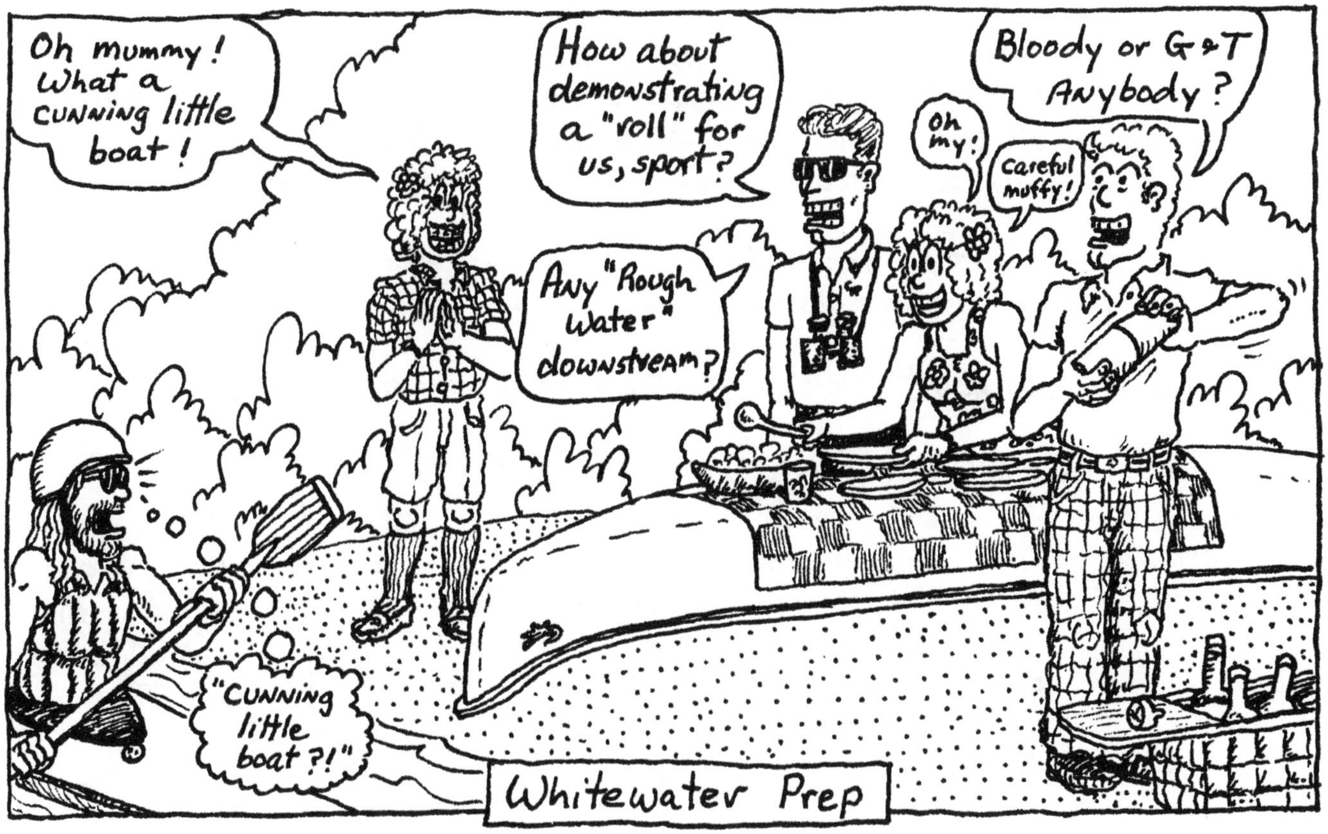
Oh mummy! What a cunning little boat!
How about demonstrating a "roll" for us, sport?
Oh my!
Bloody or G&T Anybody?
Careful muffy!
Any "Rough water" downstream?
"CUNNING little boat?!"
Whitewater Prep

Glossary, slang terms, and terminology

backender - a reverse ender. The boat stands vertically on the stern end instead of the bow end.

bad - good (although sometimes "bad" is bad.

boat scouting - inspecting a rapid from your boat by eddy-hopping and running it in stages.

boulder - extra big rock (refrigerator size and up).

boulder garden - a rapid or shoal ornamented with lots of boulders.

canoe - A.K.A. "open boat." - an elongated symmetrical river craft usually paddled by one or two people using single-bladed paddles. A canoe with a deck is referred to as a "decked canoe".

canoeist - see "C-boater" or "open boater"

C-boat - decked canoe - A.K.A. "pain boat", see "C-boater".

C-boater - Depending on your perspective, C-boaters are either the most highly skilled form of boater or the most highly masochistic. On the river C-boaters look like kayakers with canoe paddles, on shore they are usually limping or completely unable to walk.

cfs - "cubic feet per second" - A.K.A. "cubes" - refers to the volume of water passing an established point of reference on a river.

creek - A.K.A. "run", "crick", - a diminutive river.

crunchola - What happens when you hit a rock.

decked canoe - A single-person decked canoe is referred to as a "C-1", a two-person decked canoe is a "C-2".

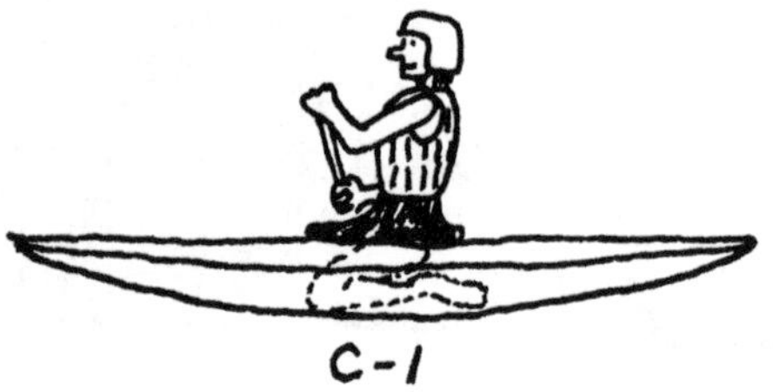

C-1

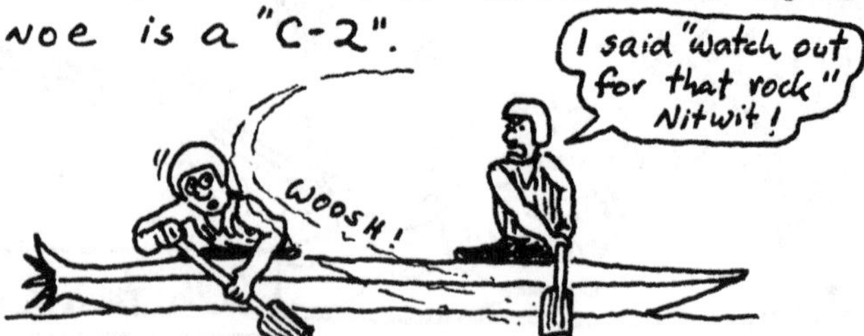
WOOSH!
I said "watch out for that rock" Nitwit!

Drop - Any vertical change in the riverbed that is perpendicular. Drops higher than six feet are frequently called "waterfalls".

dynamic - As in "dynamic peel-out", "dynamic eddy", etc. Used to describe an extreme form of anything. Dynamic lunch stop ?!

eat it - to flip over or take a nasty swim. Variations include: "chewed", "body-surfed", "creamed", "crunched", "douched", "eaten", "mangled", "mashed," "munched", "mutilated", "puréed", "stuffed", "thrashed", "trashed", "woofed", etc.

eddy - The relatively calm spots found on the downstream side of rocks, pilings, etc. Normally eddies are good places to be, but on a floodstage river they can become whirlpools or bizarre boat traps

eddy fence - high water phenomenon usually. The eddy line becomes a violent hole-like mess that can eat boats and swimmers.

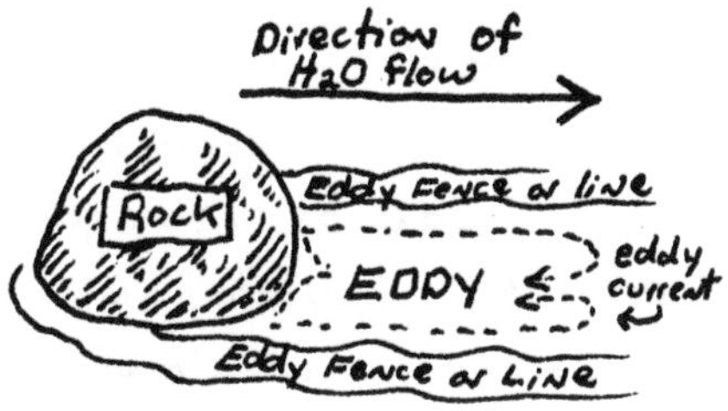

Direction of H_2O flow
Rock
Eddy Fence or line
EDDY
eddy current
Eddy Fence or Line

eddy line - the interface of the downstream flow and the eddy current. The wet version of wind shear.

ender - Aka "pop up", "endo", - standing the boat on end in holes or on waves. A good ender is when the boat gets stood perpendicular to the river and shot completely out of the water. A great ender is when you and your boat land in a raft. See "backender" and "pirouette".

entrapment - Getting trapped in or out of your boat in moving H_2O. This is generally an ultra-serious life-threatening situation requiring instantaneous rescue. Entrapment is avoided in most cases by always scouting rapids, avoiding blind drops and strainers, and never ever walking and/or dragging your feet in fast-moving water.

Articles on entrapment rescue techniques can be found in the AWA Journal and the River Safety Task Force Newsletter - read them!

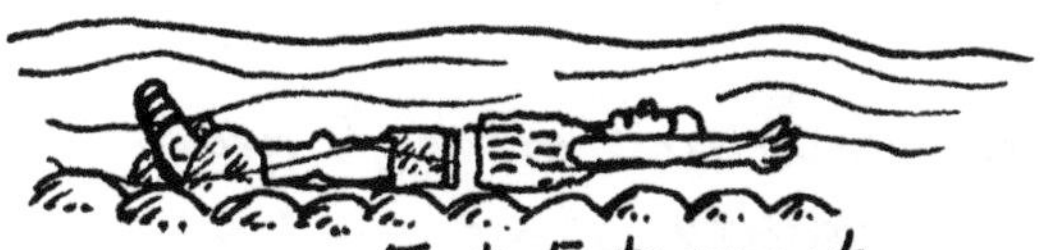

Foot Entrapment

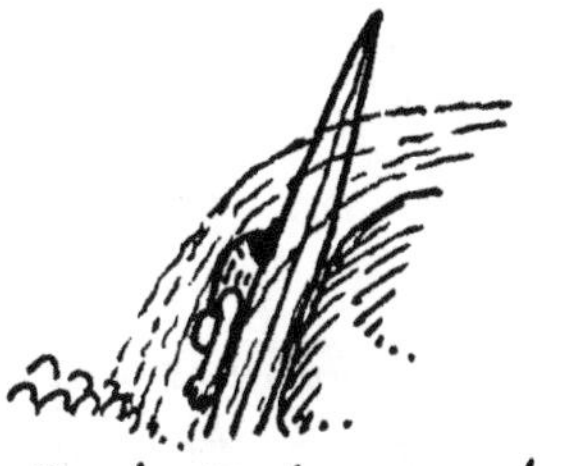

Boat Entrapment

Eskimo Roll - A self-rescue technique used by decked (and open!) boaters. Rolling is done by executing a series of upside-down underwater paddle strokes which, with the correct body-english, usually results in an upright (and happy) boater.

①
②
Eskimo Roll
③
④

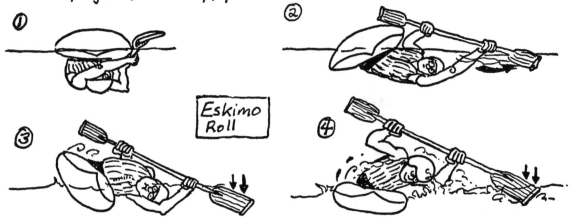

Expert boater - Usually a self-conferred title [see "S&M Products"], the qualifications for "expert" are nebulous and vary regionally. An "expert boater" can be: Any competent boater, Anyone who paddles the Gauley and lives, Anyone who owns or works in a whitewater specialty store, any river guide, any raft guide, any outfitter and/or anyone who makes maps of rivers or writes river guidebooks.

Falls - aka "waterfall" - Any vertical drop higher than six feet.

Flat Water - Any water that is still or flows in a sluggish manner. The bane of whitewater boaters, flat water is actually paddled for "fun" in some parts of the country !?

Flat water as perceived by WW boaters
Argh!
Whitewater
Flat Water

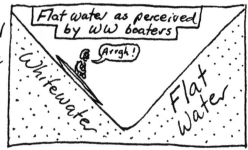

Funny water - Usually anything but. Funny water is mostly found on high-volume or floodstage rivers and manifests itself as whirlpools percolating eddies, exploding waves, mobile eddy fences, etc.

gradient - Refers to the steepness of the riverbed. Gradient is commonly expressed as the drop in feet-per-mile average.

Hair - A river or creek possessing a combination of high gradient, high volume, and extreme technical difficulty. Hair or "hairy" are also descriptive terms for any rapid, hole, etc. that is profoundly frightening / dangerous.

helmet - Aka. "beanie", "hat", "brain bucket" - rigid head protection device.

hero route - Most difficult imaginable route through a rapid

hole - see "hydraulic"

hot dog - Extraordinarily acrobatic boater or a beginner with a death wish.

Hydraulic - AKA. "hole", "sousehole", "vertical eddy", "keeper", "reversal". Hydraulics are caused by water flowing over an obstacle and creating a recirculating flow. Hydraulics come in an infinite variety and are a source of amusement and/or fear for boaters. A hole used as an eddy is referred to as a "keeper eddy".

Kayak - A.k.a. "yak", "K-1", "river volkswagon" - The most common decked river-craft and the easiest decked boat to master. Kayaks are highly maneuverable, fast, and require a moderate degree of skill to paddle. Most kayakers sit in the boat and use a two-bladed paddle.

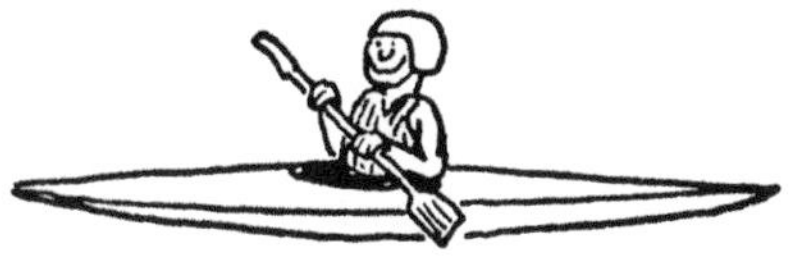
Kayak

Kayaker - Anyone who paddles (or attempts to paddle) a kayak. From the point of view of non-paddlers, kayakers are generally perceived to be Ⓐ the whitewater equivalent of Hells Angels, or Ⓑ brain-damaged river loonies, or both. Easily recognized on the river, kayakers tend to travel in large groups and engage in bizarre rituals in each and every rapid. Kayakers tend to view all other types of rivercraft as slow-moving obstacles to wave/hole playing, with rafts being most disliked of all. Canoes are tolerated as amusing entertainment and/or comic relief, particularly when a swamping or spill occurs. Decked canoeists [see "C-boater"] seem to be universally disliked and distrusted by kayakers. "Rumbles" between kayakers an C-boaters are not uncommon in the Southeast. Never call a kayaker a "kayakist" or a "feelthy two-blader", at least to his face.

local(s) - Recognized by "Goin' fishin'?" or "What's that, a ski?" and similar questions. Locals are the people indigenous to whatever area you happen to be in. Generally friendly when treated with respect. Locals in mountain areas tend to look upon whitewater boating as an activity somewhere between devil worship and heroin addiction.

open boater - A.k.a. "canoeists", "canoers" - Anyone who paddles an open canoe. Easily recognizable for their proclivity for swimming class 4 rapids and thinking it's fun. Often heard saying "shit, that's _easy_ with two blades".

peelout - pulling out of an eddy pointed upstream. When you cross the eddy line the downstream current snatches the bow of the boat and spins the boat abruptly 180° and you're facing downstream - that is unless you forgot to lean downstream - say "hi!" to the trout.

pillow - a cushion of water on the upstream face of a rock or boulder. Can be braced into in tight situations.

pin - see "entrapment"

pirouette - An ender with a half-twist... You pivot the standing boat with a crossdraw and land facing downstream.

pool - a calm area just below a rapid.

put in - The place where you park the car and get in your boat.

raft - A.k.a. "rubber bus", "pig boat", "barge" etc. An inflatable rubber boat used mainly by commercial outfitters. The one good thing about a raft is the vast quantity of beer and food it can carry.

raft guide - aka. "guide", "boatman" - the man or woman in charge of the raft. Raft guides typically come in two varieties - the jocks and the crazies. They can also be classified by region - West of the Mississippi you find the Western Boat Toad and, naturally, in the East you find the Eastern Boat Toad. Fun people, mostly.

rafters - a.k.a. "breeders", "customers" etc. [see "turkey"] Rafters are typically middle-class caucasian professionals who think whitewater was designed and built by Walt Disney. Life is one big E-ride... wa-hoo! Often resented by private boaters, rafters do provide some of us with occasional free lunches, money, and some great cartoon material.

rapid - a section of river characterized by increased gradient, fast water, waves and/or holes, rocks, and assorted other obstacles. There is a controversy in the higher echelons of the W.W. community regarding the use of "rapid" as opposed to "rapids". The plurality advocates insist that the singular form "rapid" isn't even found in the dictionary! Sorry guys - "Rapid" singular is right there under "R" in both Webster's and the Oxford English Dictionary.

river left - on the left facing downstream. Since most all rivers flow in only one direction, the downstream orientation eliminates lots of confusion. see "river right".

river right - on the right facing downstream.

rock garden - a rapid or shoal ornamented with numerous rocks.

roll - a small loaf of bread, usually baked - similar to a muffin or biscuit.

roostertail - A fountain-like liquid obstacle caused by fast-moving water striking a rock and spewing in an upwardly direction.

safety rope - a.k.a. "throw rope", "rescue rope", "rapid floss" - An essential piece of river running equipment, safety rope(s) should accompany any group down any river! Also great for impromtu boat-thief lynchings!

Scouting - to visually inspect a rapid, drop, etc. from the shore.

shoal - a nebulous term referring to anything from a rock garden to a gravel bar. Usually a shallow ledgy section with fast water and lots of obstacles to hang up on.

shuttle - What you do before and after the river trip. This involves putting some type of vehicle at the takeout so you can retrieve the vehicle you left at the put in.

Slide show - Common weekend ritual for paddlers with nowhere to go. For females and non-paddlers, the normal whitewater slide show is roughly equivalent to an overdose of Valium or Thorazine.

sneak - to take the easiest (or safest) route thru a rapid. Can also mean to covertly portage a rapid. A.K.A. "chicken route", "tourist route," "girl scout route". See "hero route".

speared - A.K.A. "harpooned"- Being speared is getting stabbed by either the bow or stern of a decked boat. Commonly occurring in eddies and on surfing waves, getting speared is roughly the equivalent of being run over by a U.P.S. truck.

stopper - Either a hole or breaking wave that stops you dead.

strainer - Any obstacle in the river that allows water to pass through but not boats and people. Fallen trees, wire, fence, debris, etc. can be extremely dangerous and should always be given a wide berth whenever possible.

surf - to ride a wave on its upstream face or to play in a hole (intentionally or unintentionally). Hole surfing is easier than wave surfing because once you get in the hole, it does all the work.

take out - The place where you get out of the boats and into the cars.

tuber - A.K.A. "Hole Bait", "Dead Meat", [see "Turkey"]. A tuber is a root-like vegetable and/or someone who runs rivers in an inner tube, usually without the benefit of helmet, lifejacket, and common sense. Despite the charming egalitarian aspects of the "sport", tubing is proof that natural selection is still at work. The tuber of the future will be scarce but probably quite strong. Improvement in intelligence is not likely.

turkey - [see "rafter", "tuber",] Generic term for novice boaters, rafters, and tubers. To expert boaters it describes everyone else. Variations include: bozo, nebbish, neednoid, pinhead, touroid, yahoo, etc.

tweeze - A.K.A. "Thread the Needle" - to take a tight route through two or more obstacles. Also may mean to catch a tiny seam between two holes.

walk the dog - to portage a rapid, drag your boat, or covertly indulge in controlled substances.

wave - You know what a wave is.

undercut rock - a rock, boulder, or rock formation that has been eroded just beneath the surface of the water. Undercut can also refer to a submerged overhanging rock. Radical undercutting can result in a mushroom-like configuration with the base of the "cap" just under the surface. Extremely dangerous for paddlers, undercut rocks are often jammed with logs and other river debris, creating nasty undercut strainers!

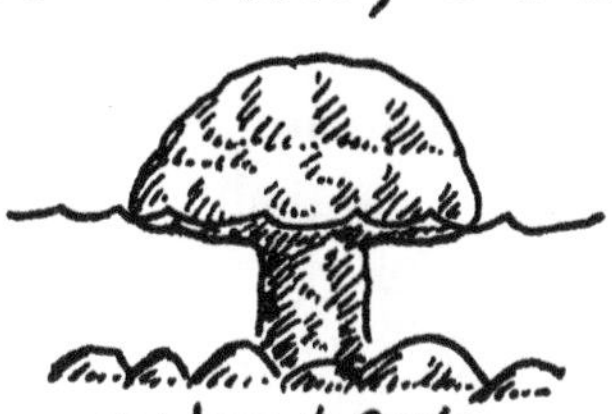

Undercut Rock

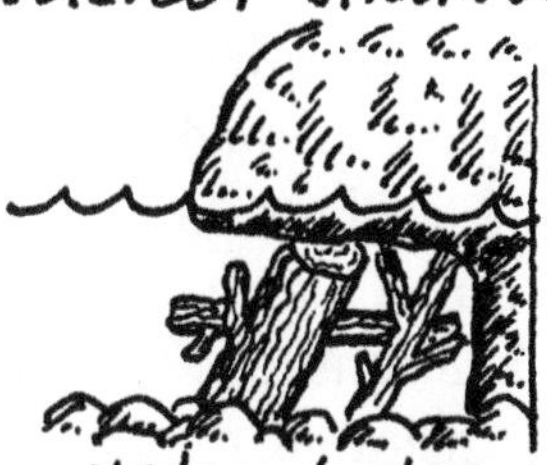

Undercut strainer

Zoo - A.K.A. "E-ride", "Six Flags Over Neoprene" - Term used to describe any particularly crowded or overcommercialized river or rapid. Examples: Swimmers Rapid-Yok, Ocoee on any summer weekend, New River Gorge between 11:00 AM and 2:00 PM, etc.

ABOUT THE AUTHOR

William "Not Bill" Nealy was a wild, gentle, brilliant artist and creator turned cult hero who wrote 10 books for Menasha Ridge Press from 1982 to 2000. William shared his hard-won "crash-and-learn" experiences through humorous hand-drawn cartoons and illustrated river maps that enabled generations to follow in his footsteps. His subjects included paddling, mountain biking, skiing, and inline skating. His hand-drawn, poster-size river maps of the Nantahala, Ocoee, Chattooga, Gauley, Youghiogheny, and several other rivers are still sought after and in use today.

William was born in Birmingham, Alabama. He and his wife, Holly Wallace, spent their adult years in a home William built in the woods on the outskirts of Chapel Hill, North Carolina, along with an assortment of dogs, lizards, pigs, snakes, turtles, and amphibians. William died in 2001.

His longtime friend and publisher, Bob Sehlinger, wrote: "When William Nealy died in 2001, paddling lost its poet laureate, one of its best teachers, and its greatest icon. William was arguably the best-known ambassador of whitewater sport, entertaining and instructing hundreds of thousands of paddlers through his illustrated books, including the classics: *Whitewater Home Companion Volumes I and II, Whitewater Tales of Terror, Kayaks to Hell,* and his best-known work, *Kayak,* which combined expert paddling instruction with artful caricatures and parodies of the whitewater community itself."

You can learn more about William, his art, and his many books at thewilliamnealy.com.

photo: MAGPIE